BILLY CASPER: *Winner*

BILLY
CASPER:
Winner

Paul D. Peery

PRENTICE-HALL, INC., ENGLEWOOD CLIFFS, N.J.

To my beloved
D. K. P.
who gave so much toward this book

FOREWORD

Reading *Billy Casper: Winner* is quite a bit like going over an old scorecard of a well-remembered round, or as we golf professionals say, a career round of golf. Surprisingly, the little things are recalled every bit as vividly as the momentous moments in this penetrating biography.

The accuracy of this work is especially gratifying. I am thankful for this accuracy because of the wonderful recollections that can again be enjoyed—like the keenly anticipated Sunday breakfast that was "Steak Day" during my early years on my grandfather's ranch in New Mexico. Even Grandma's limp, which proximity and youth caused me to overlook, came back to mind.

Author Paul D. Peery has seen fit to have the book cover five facets of my life: (1) my formative years, (2) my health problems, (3) my golfing career, (4) my spiritual life, and (5) my future. I cannot but marvel at the skilled precision of this exploration.

Too much has been written—often facetiously—about my exotic diet of buffalo, elephant and hippopotamus steak. I, therefore, am glad to see an honest appraisal of Dr. Theron Randolph's wonderful work; it wasn't simply a glamorous diet, but a vitally needed health program which ultimately saved my golfing career.

I was ramming down loads of aspirin tablets weekly in hopes of alleviating a constant and excruciatingly painful headache. My hands would puff up, leaving me with the touch of a blacksmith on the greens, where, by reputation, I was supposed to be most skilled as a putter.

Even though I went to bed early at night, I had difficulty sleeping and the next morning I would be tired and even sleepy after only a few holes of play. I admittedly was cross and sometimes downright surly, a condition perhaps brought about by my inability to comprehend this strange, strength-sapping sensation.

It was only the excitement and thrill of the contest with "Mr. Par" and my fellow professionals that enabled me to fulfill my daily assignments on the golf course. It is significant that during this period I had the worst years of my career.

My achievements on the golf course have been considerably chronicled in the news media. However, I would not be honest with myself if I didn't say that I enjoyed having the opportunity to relive one of the greatest moments of my career. This occurred when I was fortunate enough to overcome a seven-stroke deficit in only eight holes to tie one of the greatest golfers of all time, Arnold Palmer, in the USGA National Open in San Francisco. The next day in an 18-hole playoff for the most coveted title in golf, I again was fortunate to come from behind to beat my good friend, Arnie, for my second National Open Championship.

I honestly feel that too much has been written and said about my spiritual life without enough understanding of what it means to me. It never was my intention to pretend that I was a "goody-goody." I can only say that my religion since joining the Church of Jesus Christ of Latter-day Saints has proved to be a source of great personal inspiration and strength and a warm, encompassing bond with my family. This book presents the picture more faithfully.

If I could add anything to this excellent work, it would be to stress even more the roles of my wife Shirley and of her mother, Dorothy, whom Shirley and I fondly call Granny. I seriously doubt that my career and, more importantly, my life, could have progressed to its current station without them.

What about my future in golf? Very frankly, I feel, despite my modest accomplishments, that I still haven't reached the peak of my game. Fortunately, I have good health, I have honed my competitive edge and my business affairs are being totally handled by competent colleagues, especially the new director of my activities, Ed Barner of Uni-Managers, Inc., so that now I can concentrate fully on golf.

I intend to compete much more in distant lands to test other people's courses and competition. As for goals, well, they just suddenly develop. For example, when I was fortunate enough to amass $205,168 in prize money winnings in 1968, golf writers said this was the all-time money winnings record. Suddenly, the PGA said that Jack Nicklaus had the record with $211,566, even though for ten months previously the PGA had announced Jack's winnings as $188,998. (A writer friend said on his radio show, "Billy Casper should demand at least an asterisk.") My reaction? Fine, it'll give me something to shoot at next year.

BILLY CASPER

CONTENTS

ONE

"ALL THAT CRAZY MEAT"

The delivery truck rushed along the highway that cut through Bonita Valley. Steve MacKenzie, the driver, pulled out his bill of lading and grinned. All that crazy meat!

He read the first item: "3 rump roasts, hippopotamus." His grin broadened. What kind of a guy would eat such stuff? And the next item: "Ground elephant." Ugh! He *knew* what kind of a guy ate that meat. Billy Casper, number-one golfer, 1966. Second-highest money-winner of all time on the professional circuit.

Steve put the bill of lading back in his pocket. He'd sure played in luck today. These shipments of exotic meats had been coming in to Casper for two years now, but this was the first time he'd ever been lucky enough to deliver it. Ordinarily his route lay out La Jolla way. But today the South Bay man was sick and Steve had jumped at the chance. Billy

1

Casper was just about tops in his book. Steve had wanted to meet him ever since Billy had won the U.S. Open in 1959. His son, Douglas, was also a great fan of Billy's. Douglas was fourteen, a Junior Golfer, and he followed the game like some kids followed slot-car racing. Billy Casper was his idol. Billy wasn't the only golfer in the San Diego area—there was Gene Littler and Phil Rogers—but Doug's eyes got that starry look only for Casper. And now that he, Steve, was delivering this crazy meat to the Caspers', maybe he'd get to see Billy. If his luck held he might even have an opportunity to ask him for his autograph. For Douglas, of course. Autograph-hunting was a kid's game.

The truck rumbled its way through the sleepy village of Bonita while Steve looked for some monument to Casper. Then his grin widened once more. What had he expected to find—a statue? Billy holding a putter aloft? Or his face raised, arms at the top of his stroke, his gaze on the far-distant ball he'd just sent screaming down the fairway? Something inspirational, sure. He thought Billy Casper was just about the greatest guy in the whole game. And maybe he'd see him in a few minutes. He'd keep a sharp lookout so he could tell Doug all about it.

The truck reached Palm Drive, and when Steve turned right he faced a signboard with the names of the owners of the houses on the hill. He scanned the nameplates. Yes, there it was in the lower-left corner: "W. E. Casper." What'd the *E* stand for? The truck continued up the hill, the road unwinding between double rows of palms. Once more a grin came over Steve's face. What other kind of tree had he expected on Palm Drive?

At the top he came out on a flat turn-around and gazed in awe at the large Spanish-type house. Twenty-two rooms, an article had said. His heart speeded up as he went to the back door. He pressed the chime button and the door opened. A pretty young woman of about thirty smiled at him.

"Hello," she said. "Is it the meat?"

"Mrs. Casper?" Steve asked. Her voice was like music, he thought.

Shirley Casper nodded. "Just bring it in the kitchen, will you?"

Steve returned to the truck, unloaded a crate onto the dolly, then started for the house again. Shirley held the door while he reversed to back the dolly up the steps and down the short hall into an all-white kitchen, where he looked around, recording the occasion for later storytelling. "Sure is a swell kitchen, Mrs. Casper," he said. "My wife would go crazy after that island in the middle there."

Shirley tossed her head in a characteristic gesture that meant she was pleased. "We like it," she said simply. "Put the bigger packages on the counter, will you? It's easier for me to store it in the freezer if it's already lifted. I have to do it myself today. The maid's off."

"I could help if you want," Steve offered quickly.

"Sure you can spare the time?"

"Oh yeah," Steve lied. "I'm in no hurry."

He went back to the truck for another carton. Three times he made the trip, each dolly load piling high in the immaculate kitchen. His glance swept over the two electric ovens and the nine-burner electric stove. Then he spotted the refrigerators.

"Three iceboxes?" he asked in disbelief.

Shirley's laugh bounced merrily around the room. "No, just two. The other is a freezer. And we have two more freezers and another refrigerator out in the areaway."

Steve's eyes widened. When the Caspers did things, they did 'em big. "Three freezers and three iceboxes," he said.

"We need them all," Shirley answered. "This game meat, for instance."

Steve paused in his unloading to glance at a label: ANTELOPE STEW. "What does this taste like? And does everybody like it?"

A bright-eyed young girl of about thirteen came into the kitchen. "I like it, but my brothers don't," she stated.

"This is Linda," Shirley said. "My oldest."

Steve gazed at the sweet pixie-face. Mischief there, he thought. But under control. Could stir up a tempest without much trouble.

Linda picked up his bill of lading. "Any whale this time?" she asked. "I don't like whale. It's too greasy."

"It just *sounds* fat, doesn't it?" Shirley agreed. "I always think of blubber when I see the meat, though I never tasted blubber."

Steve stripped open the last carton. How could he stall for more time? Then he saw a copy of *Sports Illustrated* on the counter. The cover featured a picture of Billy in a yellow sweater and red shirt. To the lower right stood a glass of milk. Billy's hand rested on a replica of a roast of buffalo. Steve picked up the magazine and said, "Sure is a good picture."

"Yes," Linda agreed. "And there's an article about Daddy, too."

He'd get a copy. Douglas would be pleased.

The back door burst open and two boys raced in, the elder carrying a muddy football, the younger shouting after him.

"Mommy, Billy won't give me my football," Bobby cried. "Daddy and me were playing and Billy took off with the ball."

"Daddy and *I*," Shirley corrected automatically.

Hotly, the elder boy came to his own defense. "But Daddy promised to play with me."

"I'm sure he'll play with both of you," Shirley cut in. "Now, Billy, you give Bobby back his ball." She turned again to Steve. "Bill loves to play football with the boys."

Steve nodded. He could see that Billy was great on family. He put down the copy of *Sports Illustrated*. "Well, I guess I better mosey," he said in regret.

Shirley noticed his hesitation. "My husband will be here in

just a moment," she offered. "Wonder he's not here already. He can't stay away when packages arrive."

Bobby strutted forward. "My daddy's the best golf-ball player in the whole world," he stated firmly.

Steve grinned at the wording. A smart kid. Good-looking, too. Whole family was good-looking. He sure would like to see Billy, but he'd already stayed longer than he should have.

The back door opened a second time and a smiling man came in. For an instant Steve was awed, but then the kindness in the face, the friendly smile, the twinkling eyes, put him at ease.

Young Billy dashed across the room. "Daddy, you said you'd play with *me*," he complained.

Billy ruffled his son's hair. "How can anyone play if you swipe the ball?" He crossed the kitchen and scanned the packages of meat. "Any rabbit?" he asked.

"You know we buy rabbit locally," Shirley answered. "This is just the game meat."

"Rabbit's the best."

Billy sure had lost weight, Steve thought. At the Open in 1959 he must have weighed 225. But now he couldn't be more than 175. Was that what the diet did? Make him lose weight? What impact did all this crazy meat have on the guy? And on his family? Because Billy sure was a family man. Just look at him love his son. It took a family to make a man.

"I got a son," Steve said. "Name's Douglas. He's a fan of yours, Mr. Casper. He's a Junior Golfer."

Billy's eyes glowed.

"Mind if I ask you something?" Steve went on.

"Shoot," Bill answered, stuffing one hand in his pocket, the other cuddling young Billy's head against him.

"You sure lost a lot of weight," Steve said. "That what your diet's for? To make you lose weight?" He indicated the last package, marked ELK, which Shirley was just putting into the freezer.

"No," she called over her shoulder. "We're on a special

program. It hasn't anything to do with weight, though Bill has lost on it." She shut the freezer door. "It's an allergy program. We have to avoid certain foods, and the only way we can achieve our rotation is to have game meat."

"Rotation?" Steve asked, puzzled.

"Granny ought to be here," Billy broke in. "She knows more about the program than anyone else."

"Granny's helping at her church today," Linda explained. "She'll be back soon."

"Well, I can tell you about it," Shirley broke in, slightly miffed. "I know about it, too."

Steve smiled. Women were all the same, whether they were wives of golf pros or expressmen. No other woman could do something better than they could. Not even their own mothers.

"When we first went to Dr. Randolph," Shirley began, "Bill complained he always felt bad after breakfast. And no wonder. He found out he was allergic to all the things he usually ate for breakfast. Orange juice, eggs, bacon, any pork—oh, all the breakfast things."

"You mean he broke out or something?"

"Oh no. Not just the hives or such. Allergy is chemical imbalance. It can be inherited. Or acquired. You eat toast every day for breakfast and you're apt to develop wheat allergy."

"But I eat toast, and I never had—"

"You don't know," Shirley broke in. "D'you ever sniffle in the morning? Or sneeze maybe? Or hack your throat?"

"Well, sure. Most every day. But we always call it post-nasal drip."

"You ever moody?" Shirley persisted. "Temperamental?"

"Sometimes," he admitted.

"Uh huh. Allergic."

"Honey," Billy interrupted. "We better let the man go. He has other deliveries to make."

Steve checked himself. He'd forgotten about the autograph.

Mr. Casper plainly wanted him out, so he started down the hall. Doug sure would be disappointed.

"Well, good-bye, folks. And good luck on tour, Mr. Casper," he said.

"Wait a minute," Billy said, picking up the *Sports Illustrated*. "What'd you say your boy's name was?"

Steve's eyes lighted up. "Douglas," he answered. "Doug MacKenzie."

Billy took a pen from the kitchen desk and scribbled on the magazine, then handed it to Steve. "Here," he said. "Take this to him for me."

Steve looked at the picture and felt a lump in his throat. Across the page, Billy had written: *To Doug MacKenzie, from Billy Casper.*

TWO
BOYHOOD

The man was a boy.

One quiet Sunday morning in the fall of 1936, young Billy Earl Casper raced barefoot down the road from his daddy's New Mexico house to that of his grandfather. Of course, he reasoned, it really was his grand*parents'*. Grandma lived there, too, but somehow he always thought of it as Grandpa's house. Grandpa was so *big*. It seemed the house was a part of him, not him a part of the house. Yep. Grandpa was a big, big man. And when he, Billy Earl, grew up, he wanted to be like him. People all over Grant County respected him. Asked his ideas on whatever troubled them. People *came* to Grandpa—even though he scared them to death at first. His voice was so loud.

An early-Sunday-morning quiet can be shattered by a little boy, particularly if he has something on his mind. Sound and

movement punctuated Billy Earl's arrival at his grandparents' farmhouse. The screen door smacked sharply, bare feet
thudded in staccato succession across the porch, and the heavy
back door banged shut behind him. He stopped, emerging
from noise into Grandpa's hushed version of Sunday morning.
Solemn, he gazed from Grandma, standing meekly by her
range, to his grandpa, spread out on a chair beside the kitchen
table. Grandpa did not look up from his reading. But Billy
Earl could see he was expected. His place was set, and
Grandma smiled at him.

Even now Grandpa did not look up. "What's your hurry,
boy?"

"We're gonna play, Grandpa. The first time on our new
course." Billy Earl shifted from one foot to the other. "The
cows is done with. And I helped. And Daddy's comin' too.
Let's go, Grandpa."

Slowly Grandpa turned his head sideways just enough to
squint a look at his grandson. "Don't you know it's eatin'
time?" he demanded.

"Aw, Grandpa—"

Billy Earl paused. Even at just-five, the boy understood
that Grandpa did not relinquish the important things like
eating and reading, and visiting, not for anything at all. Not
even for the new golf course they had made. Billy Earl
pushed one foot hard against the floor and curled his big toe
under. He felt a redness spread over his face. But he said
nothing. Eating time. He relaxed. It wasn't such a bad idea.
Suddenly he discovered he was plenty hungry. For the first
time the breakfast smells from Grandma's stove reached him.
Potatoes frying, meat—yes, and flannel cakes. Important as
the new golf course was to him this morning, Billy Earl decided it was a pretty good idea to eat first. Anyway, Grandpa
would never let him out until he did.

"Well, okay." With a trace of reluctance the boy moved
slowly toward the chair Grandpa indicated.

"Sunday's steak mornin' at this house, Billy Earl," Grandpa

said. "Feller's got to eat if he's gonna do his best." Grandpa
waddled his huge jowls in conviction. "Get some of them
flannel cakes over here to this golfer, Bertha," he commanded
loudly. "How's it come you're so slow this mornin'? Get the
boy some of that steak while you're about it. And *be* about it."

Billy Earl grinned. Grandpa barked real loud, but he didn't
bite much. Even so, Grandma reddened, and her smile turned
into a scowl. She muttered, but no words came as she limped
from stove to table. Glaring briefly at her husband, she set the
plate of cakes down.

Grandpa was old country and Early American-German.
His home and family attitudes were pure Prussian. And
Grandma resisted only partly. She sputtered, but did what he
said. He was the dominant figure. And he domineered. Grandma's partial resistance created a mild flurry, nothing more.
Outwardly the man ignored his wife's annoyance, but it
teased him into a greater tyranny.

"All right now, woman. Get that steak over to us. And
don't overcook it. You been doin' terrible." He squinted
dourly. "I don't cotton to dry steak. You know that."

Billy Earl ignored his grandparents' argument. He'd heard
the noise of it many times. He took a big mouthful of flannel
cakes. Grandma really was a good cook, no matter what
Grandpa said. And Grandpa knew it.

"Well, Bertha?" Grandpa's tone was harsh.

Grandma clattered her pancake turner to the floor, but she
delivered the steak. Grandpa lowered his first chin into his
second and sat back a bit.

"Humph! Looks dry's a buffalo chip," he commented.

Grandma's complexion became more purple than red. The
mock in his pained expression eluded her.

"William Adolph, I sometimes wish you was dead. Completely dead!" Bitterness coated her high-pitched voice.

Grandpa's eyes returned to their normal squint. He frowned
briefly, glancing down at the pancake turner on the floor.
Then his large face creased into a strange grin.

"Well, Bertha m'dear, when I do die, I hope it's with a full stomach." His laugh was a series of loud snorts. Then his glance warmed and he put up his hand to rest it on her arm. "It's real good—*Grandma*," he said softly.

The sound of the word brought a suffused pleasure to her cheeks, removing the upset. Grandpa laughed again, a warm, friendly laugh.

"Never forget, Billy Earl," he chortled. "That's what our name means. 'Casper' means a clown, a cut-up. Live up to it, m'boy. Good for your liver." Again his chortle filled the room.

At the difference in tone, Billy Earl glanced up from the important business of eating. "Okay," he said. "Grandma, I like your cooking. I bet the steak's good." He glanced at the center of argument. He still didn't have his piece. "Can I have some?"

"Here, boy." Grandpa shoved the platter across the table. "Help yourself."

The screen door slapped and heavy footsteps creaked on the porch. Earl appeared in the doorway, and Grandma returned to her stove.

"Better finish up, son," Earl advised. "Things to do this morning."

"Now hold on there. Don't you interfere with the boy's eatin'," Grandpa bellowed. Then, as if there had been no rebuke, he added cordially, "Good mornin', Earl." He glanced down at the golf club in the younger man's hand. "I see you made it short some."

Billy Earl frowned.

"Yes, Papa," Earl answered. "I had it done in Silver City. It'll be better for him this way." He held out a cut-down five-iron.

"Bring Earl a plate, Bertha," Grandpa ordered.

Earl glanced at Billy Earl but said nothing. The boy chewed methodically, slowly, his frown deepening. He'd lost interest in his food. He glanced at the club in his father's hand, then slid off his chair. He darted to the door and was out before his grandfather could call him back. In a moment, to the accompaniment of banging doors and plop-plopping bare feet, he returned carrying a full-sized five-iron. His dad's.

"I'm goin' to use this one, Daddy," he announced. He stood erect, staring up at his father, shirt and jeans parted, exposing three inches of bare stomach, his pudgy jaw still pocked with food and set in a firm line. His smaller version of Grandpa's straight, strong nose pointed upward with the tilting of his chin.

Earl reached for the club. "What you plan to do with that?"

Billy Earl tightened his small hands around the shaft. A telltale welling of tears glistened in his deep blue eyes.

"That club's as big as you are, Billy Earl," Grandma said softly.

"No," the boy disagreed. "Looky." He held it upright in front of his face. The top of the grip came just to the tip of his nose.

"You keep out of this, Bertha," Grandpa commanded loudly. He turned to Billy Earl. "Give that to me."

"No," the boy answered. He blinked once, but his expression remained unchanged.

Earl started to take off his belt. Grandma frowned and moved forward.

Ignoring her, Grandpa repeated, "Give that to me."

The boy stood in silence, holding firmly to the club. If he trembled in his heart, nothing showed.

Earl doubled the belt in his hand. He grabbed the boy and jerked him nearer.

In fury, Grandma shouted, "William Adolph, I swear you'd put your head through a buzzsaw afore you'd change your mind 'bout anything." She paused, then smiled as her anger softened. "And it kinda begins to look like there's another Casper the very same way."

Billy Earl waited in defiant but respectful rebellion. For a moment everything went silent again, and even motion seemed suspended. At the risk of revealing his wall eye, Grandpa stared in open-eyed amazement. Then he grinned quizzically, and the room relaxed. He put an arresting arm out toward Earl. And with a man-to-man gesture he put his other arm around Billy Earl's shoulder.

Earl stared, astonished. "You ain't goin' to wop him?" he demanded.

Grandpa shook his head. He turned Billy Earl's taut face toward his own. "You figure you can do better with this club than the other'n?"

The boy's reply was matter-of-fact. "Yes, sir."

"What's so good about this one, I wonder?" Grandpa asked.

"It's Daddy's," Billy Earl answered.

The two men looked at each other, at the boy, then again at each other. Earl's face had reddened with pleasure.

"Tell you what, Billy Earl," Grandpa said gravely. "Let's go out to the course and you just show us which club is yours."

"Okay," Billy Earl agreed, excited. "Come on, Daddy. Let's go."

This glimpse into Billy's childhood shows the boy's eager search for love, for love and a parental image. A search that was not to reach fruition for many years, not until the Church entered his life. Billy Earl loved his father, wanted very much to please him. Eagerly the boy sought a father-image upon which to mold his life. Earl taught his son golf. In fact, Earl is the only golf teacher Billy Casper has ever had. And he taught the boy card games of all kinds. But whatever light was Earl's had long before been busheled by Grandpa's fiery temperament. It wasn't Earl's fault; not many men could have stood up to Grandpa. Billy Earl was one of the few who got away with it. The grandfather-boy relation was good, was strong, though short-lived. Grandpa was a quixotic combination of love and harshness. He could tease Grandma until she cried, then make it up to her with a pat. A butcher by trade, he was outgoing, complimentary, flattering, encouraging people to do things. He believed that his children should have good character, yet within his own family he himself was a tyrant. A heavy eater, he preferred meat and potatoes, simple food, and lots of it. He liked to sit at the table and direct the preparation of the meal, sometimes to Grandma's exasperation. He insisted the children eat heartily, especially desserts. He loved his children and grandchildren very much. And he thought the cure for everything was a shot of castor oil, which he administered in large doses. Children loved him, but at the same time were in awe of him, of his size and loudness. He liked to give them things, and enslave them by his gifts. Billy Earl was his first grandchild, and his only one for five years. Pictures of Grandpa show a huge frame, 6 feet, 350 pounds. A man accustomed to being obeyed, with large jowls that firmed in hardness at any attack against his own as well as at any wrongdoing of his own. This was the man Billy Earl sought to fill the father-image vacuum, though he was unconscious of his search. This was the man who gave the boy his stubbornness, his tenacity. This was the man whose love of children shone through the surface harshness and is today reflected in Billy's love of children. In early pictures, Billy Earl even looks like Grandpa: stout. And in his eyes a distant future is evident—or the search for it. There is a budding awareness that strikes the viewer at once. It's as if Billy could see things far off, things others could not see. These early pictures are revealing glimpses of the boy on his way to the man to come.

That backyard golf course was a three-hole setup in Grandpa's large cow-pasture. The holes were about 250 yards apart. Trees and rocks made up the obstacles. Greens were from 5 to 8 feet across. "Greens" must not be taken literally; grass and water are scarce in New Mexico. The "greens" were of gravel, gravel that came from the earth, carried out by ants in the building of their nests. The pebbles were about the size of matchheads. As a putting surface, it was hardly bent grass. But young Billy Earl greeted it eagerly. Earl had built the course for himself, allowing his son to help in the design and construction. They spread out the anthills, salvaging all the gravel for greens. Then they poured gasoline down the holes to get rid of the nests. All this labor had to be accomplished between chores—Earl working at the nearby dairy and Billy Earl busy with the cows, chickens, and the livestock on the farm. At last came the Sunday they were to use the course for the first time. Secretly, Billy Earl had worked out his father's clubs, and though they were way too long for him, he knew he could hit the ball farther with the grown-up clubs. Besides, weren't they his father's? Maybe if he showed his dad that he could really play . . . And so the youngster was determined to use the adult sticks. He'd gone on secret practices with his two dogs, Minnie and Mike, a black German shepherd and a brown-spotted mongrel, respectively. The dogs couldn't get the idea at first and insisted on bringing back the ball in a fetch that brought no pat of approval.

This Sunday morning in late September contained a pleasant fall feel, a bite to the air, a certain crispness to the sunglared golden-brown fields. The scent of sage sank deep into Billy Earl's nostrils. Clutching the full-sized club, he ran ahead of the men. He passed the water trough under the algaroba tree, the light shade giving a coolness to the glistening water. As always, he stopped, bent over, and dunked his head. He loved to drink from the trough. He drank deeply, pausing now and then for breath. Grandpa and Earl caught up with him and waited, smiling tolerantly. At last he looked up, wiped his mouth with the back of his hand, and grinned.

"Water's sure good," he said. "Cool."

"Billy Earl," Grandpa chuckled. "You'll turn into a horse."

When they came to the pasture, Billy Earl scrambled under the fence—never mind the gate. He paused to watch a rabbit scamper across the field. Earl still carried the cut-down club. Suddenly Billy Earl picked up a rock and threw it. Threw it squarely at the immobile head of a sentinel ground squirrel perched on the lip of the first hole. Before the men had even seen it, Billy Earl nailed it.

"That boy's got a keen eye," Grandpa said. "Good coordination."

"Nice throw, son," Earl added.

Billy Earl's face clouded, and his voice quivered a bit as he said, "But now he's dead."

"Yup," Grandpa agreed. "Shoulda thought of that. Let's get on with the game."

Once again Earl held out the shortened club, but Billy Earl set his legs apart and braced. "Nope," he said.

"Try it," Grandpa suggested.

Billy's blue eyes fixed on Grandpa in a stubborn stare, with his chin tilted upward. It was an indomitable look, a granite look, a direct replica of Grandpa's stony glare. The older man must have thought something such as this, for after a bit he grinned his strange smile, a half-proud, half-angry smile.

"Okay, boy. Try the big one."

Earl held out a golf ball and Billy Earl took it, dropped it on the ground, and, wasting no time, addressed the ball. He was taller than other five-year-olds, and his frame was larger than that of most boys. He closed his fingers around the grip, and as he began his practice swing the club stuck out, ludicrously long. He backed away from the ball.

"Hey, Bonehead." Earl pointed to a small mound in the adobe. "Pinch some dirt together. You need a tee."

Billy Earl obeyed. Again his fingers wrapped around the grip. He held out the club, and Earl and Grandpa nearly laughed at the extended awkwardness of the eager boy and his too-long shaft. He addressed the ball without pause, then brought his arms up, beginning his backswing. The club head mounted into perfect position above his right shoulder. With tremendous force he brought his club down, the head making a sharp smack in sure contact with the ball. The white sphere flew to the right, nearly 90 yards out onto the cow-pasture fairway. For a boy, it was a long drive.

Grandpa's smile vanished, Earl's mouth dropped open. The men glanced at each other. Ignoring his gallery, the boy trudged purposefully out in the direction of his next play. The fairway was rough. As the men followed, Billy Earl appeared to be looking the situation over, briefly. Just to the right of Billy's lie stood a clump of trees. Halfway to the pin a huge rock jutted out of the adobe as an obstacle. With only a brief moment of judgment, Billy Earl made his shot, the ball sailing freely over the rock trap. Again the sturdy figure strode forward, ignoring his gallery. He sized up his lie, and at once accurately chipped his ball onto the 10-foot pebble green. Before his gallery could catch up, he one-putted.

He turned to his Grandpa. "See? I did it."

"That you did, son. That you did." Grandpa smiled broadly. "Looks like we got us a golfer, Earl."

"Looks like," Earl agreed.

Billy Earl's face shone with pride. They moved on to the second tee. The cut-down club lay abandoned on the fairway.

The boy grew bigger than other boys, quieter, with long periods of deep thought. Always the thinker, Billy Earl approached each decision of his childhood with conservative hesitation, almost diffidence. When he was twelve, his parents separated. The father-image search went on. Grandpa provided the way for a while. Earl was a vacuum image, not antagonistic but apathetic. He gave his son the inspiration and early know-how that became Billy's great gift of golf.

Both parents loved the boy, each in his own way. We've just seen the level of his father's love. His mother, Isabel, loved the boy in a different way. Hers was not an overt love, not demonstrative. Nevertheless, she gave the boy sustenance on which to build. As she says, "I taught Bill right from wrong and let him go." Though on the surface there may have been a lack of demonstrated love, underneath it required a greater love to let her son be himself. And it gave Billy a certain *intactness*, a singleness of being, of integrity, that bolstered him throughout boyhood. He still wears it today. It is the outgrowth of that vision of faraway places that may be noted in boyhood pictures. That sight of things others do not see. In Billy's eyes today, there is a blue depth that is friendly, but which still preserves the inner man for spiritual purposes. Often, people think of him as aloof, as reserved, when actually he is just thinking other thoughts, and thinking more than most. And this is traceable to his mother's letting him go, giving him his lead, so that he could draw unto himself those strengths that steady his hand on the greens today. Those strengths make up the intactness that is the heart of Billy's character. It is his strongest motivating force. He is himself *within* himself. *Intactness.*

Don Chase, Bill's best boyhood friend, says of Bill and his parents: "Bill's Mom and Dad were divorced when I knew him in high school and they were both wonderful people. I think Bill got much of his humor from his Mom. She had explicit trust in Bill and let him make many judgments that many parents are reluctant, probably for good reason, to allow their children [to make]. She worked and was unable to be home, but Bill was more well behaved and mannered than most other kids that age. He always seemed more mature, although he was known for the fun he generated around people."

Yes, he was the product of a broken home, but he casts no blame upon it. He moved out of it, leaving it behind. No self-pity. No whining about his lack of opportunity. He created his own opportunity. Where any patterns clung that he could not comprehend, others helped him dispose of them. *But only with his permission.* Always and forever, Bill is moved only with his permission. He holds his integrity a high banner. It is his intactness.

And so the boy began to move slowly through the years, gathering to himself all that he needed to make him intact. Gathering from those around him, those who loved him. Gathering the nourishment to build the sinews that make the man.

THREE
YOUTH

On a sun-dappled fall afternoon in 1949, two teenaged girls were on their way to a Chula Vista High School football game. Shirley Ann Franklin wore a light blue sweater, a darker blue skirt, and she sparkled—"sparkled" is the word for it. Her eyes of inquisitive blue sparkled like asters in the moonlight. Her hands, ever on the move, sparkled with grace. Her swaying body, already rich with maturity, brought admiring glances and an occasional low-toned whistle from boys and appreciative and wistful smiles from older men. Her light brown hair was cut quite short, with many carefully groomed home-permanent curls that bounced as she moved. Everything about her sparkled: her voice, her laughter, her glance, her ways, all proclaimed happy youth, an attractive, popular girl on her way to a September football game with her best friend. Mary Jane Irey wore an orange sweater and a brown skirt,

21

and the contrast to Shirley's outfit enhanced the atmosphere around the two. Everything seemed cause for bubbling laughter, and their giggles were part-humor and part-Sarah Bernhardt for the benefit of the admiring boys who trailed them.

Not many ventured to whistle, however, for it was well known that Shirley didn't like that. She was not the least bit flirtatious and frowned on any overt sign of admiration, though secretly she was gratified when a boy whistled. Her mother assured people that Shirley was a "good" girl. And Shirley, though admitting this, would have acknowledged the opprobrium in the term.

In the stadium, the two girls started up toward the rest of the sophomores. On the way they passed a row of seniors, and three boys in particular turned to follow them with their glances. Outwardly, Shirley remained oblivious, but not her companion.

"Shirley, let's sit here," Mary Jane whispered, indicating the row behind the interested seniors.

Shirley shook her head. "We're supposed to sit up there," she said, moving on.

Reluctantly, Mary Jane followed. The two girls sat down with their classmates. The three senior boys huddled for a moment, then shifted to a row directly in front of the girls, while two sets of feminine shoulders moved ever so slightly in disdain.

"Boys!" Shirley said.

"Yeah," Mary Jane sympathized.

The middle senior, bigger and stouter than the others, mimicked her. "Yeah," he mocked in a falsetto.

A slight frown shadowed Shirley's face as she followed the game. Chula Vista had the ball. Suddenly a back broke free for an end run. She jumped to her feet and shouted, "Go get 'em, Team!"

"Go get 'em, Team!" shrilled the mimic.

Both girls broke into laughter. Then Mary Jane got into the act: "Yeah, Chula Vista!"

This time all three seniors sounded off: "Yeah, Chula Vista!"

The rest of the crowd picked up the cry and the typical pandemonium of youth at a football game made conversation almost impossible. Under the din, Shirley tugged at Mary Jane's sleeve. "Who's that boy?" she asked. "The one who's mocking us."

"That's Billy Casper," answered Mary Jane. "He's the best golfer in school."

Shirley's eyes went wide, and she scrutinized the boy.

Mary Jane continued. "The others are Don Chase and Jack Peacock. Bill's the S.C.I.F. golf champ."

Shirley was impressed. "Southern California Interscholastic Federation champ? Boy, he looks it. He's big." The sparkle in her eyes intensified, and into them came an odd look, a certain manipulating look, a *directive* look that would have caused her mother worry. Shirley was a very determined miss.

Neither Shirley nor Billy remembers who won that game. They don't even remember whom their Alma Mater played. But the miming—*that* they recall: the first sight of each other, the personal contact. And they recall the high-school dance that night, when they were formally introduced for the first time. Strangely enough there was no joking about the afternoon. In fact, no mention of it at all. There was practically no conversation. They danced together all evening long, and it's doubtful that either of them heard the music. This is really the story of their romance: they have been dancing together, just the two of them, all life long. It was first love for each, and the only love for both. Today, while on tour, Shirley strides along in Billy's gallery, her pace determined and rapid. And, though Billy is never aware of anyone on the course, still, he must feel the love that surrounds him every step he takes.

There was *one* small exchange of conversation at that dance: He asked to take her to a movie.

"You'll have to meet my mother," Shirley answered. But in her heart she knew her mother would approve.

"Watch this action!" Billy promised. It was a favorite remark, a sign of exuberance.

Shirley's mother has been such a profound influence on the lives of the Casper family that she should be characterized here. When Shirley first met Bill, her mother was a navy wife whose husband was on duty in the San Diego area. Dorothy Rader was a beautiful young woman, young in a way that often made people express astonishment that she was Shirley's mother. This irritated Dorothy, who was proud of her motherhood. Her grandmother had been half-Indian, half-French, and Dorothy's high cheekbones gave elegant tribute to her ancestry. Her deep blue eyes glowed with almost brown fanaticism, a zeal that her child would have the best, would be the best, and would live a God-loving life. Dorothy's strength of purpose has melded the Casper family into a unit of affection and loyalty. While Shirley watches out for Billy's well-being on tour, Dorothy guides the children in their spacious home in Bonita.

The morning after the high-school dance, as Shirley and her mother were getting ready for church, Shirley said, "I met a swell boy last night, Mama."

Dorothy rinsed the last pan. "You've lots of time for boys, Shirley." She dried her hands and turned toward the bedroom.

"But this one's special," Shirley insisted. "He's the best golfer. And he wants to take me to the movies."

Dorothy paused. "That's fine, honey. Just don't confine yourself to one boy. There's no hurry for you."

"I'd *like* to go with just one boy, if Bill was the boy."

Her mother smiled. "That's good, honey. But you'll get over it."

Shirley shook her head. And though she didn't tell her mother, she *had* told Mary Jane, right after the dance, that she was going to marry Bill.

"Marry?" Mary Jane had almost screeched. "Shirley Ann Franklin, you won't even be fifteen till next month!"

Shirley shrugged. "What's the matter? My mom married my dad when she was fifteen."

"But"—Mary Jane shifted her approach—"does *he* know anything about it?"

"Oh no," Shirley said airily. "But that doesn't make any difference. He'll know when the times comes."

No, Shirley didn't tell her mother about this conversation, but her mind was made up. And she was a *very* determined miss. And the first step toward her goal would be for Bill to meet her mother.

A few nights later the door chime sounded. Shirley was in her room, so Dorothy went to greet her future son-in-law. She swung the door wide, then stopped short. The boy standing on the threshold was tall, nearly 6 feet, and he was stout, heavy-framed, and self-possessed.

He smiled and said, "How d'you do, Ma'am?"

Impressed by his politeness and assured way, Dorothy thought, Why, he's an old man, taking my little girl out. But the boy's respectful manner soon filled her with relief and trust. She thought, Lucky us. Lucky me. And Dorothy has never had cause to regret that trust.

When the young couple prepared to leave, Dorothy noticed that Shirley's eyes were bright with adoration. And though the girl remained quiet while Bill assured Mrs. Rader they would be back on time, and that they were double-dating, Shirley's eyes danced loudly.

Thus youth began the changeover to manhood. From the stubborn boy who faced up to Grandpa Casper, Bill had grown into an equally determined young man. His search to fill the vacuum father-image, temporarily satisfied by Grandpa's massive strength, now shifted to his search for love. And he found it in the great love of his life. Accompanying this were other loves, concomitant and inclusive. One of the most important sinews that make up the man Billy Casper today is the bountiful love that became his through marriage. Not only the love of his wife, but the love of the children of that marriage, and the love of Shirley's mother.

Bill and Shirley saw a lot of each other that winter, his senior year and her sophomore. He often had dinner at her house. It was Shirley's job to wash the dishes. And even when he did not eat with them, each evening Bill would come over to dry the dishes. It was the only time in his life he helped with the dishes. Their dates were always double. And though Bill never had a car, they were lucky that his friends did. At no time did Shirley's mother become concerned. She knew she could trust them. Occasionally she would suggest that her daughter date another boy. But Shirley would have none of it. And when that *directive* look shone in the young blue eyes, her mother knew it was useless to remonstrate. There was only one requirement: Dorothy asked them never to be alone together in the house. Both were indignant.

"You don't trust us," Shirley stormed.

Bill's glance echoed her thought.

"I've never distrusted you," Dorothy answered quietly. "But promise."

Neither minded obeying the request. But both objected hotly to the apparent lack of faith. So the year passed, with love deepening and youth maturing. Billy gained stature by winning the County Amateur Tournament. Then, after his graduation, a sponsor arranged a golf scholarship to Notre Dame. Billy's mother wanted him to go. Though this was a tribute and a welcome acknowledgment, it brought sadness to the hearts of the young lovers. Then came the logical result. In August of 1950 they became engaged. They broke the news to Isabel first, for she had approved from the start. Afterward, they went to Dorothy.

The evening was warm, and the windows wide open. The fragrance of a climbing rose just outside wafted through the room. Dorothy thought the two had gone to a movie. Instead, they had gone shopping—for an engagement ring. And now they stood in the doorway, afraid to enter, yet determined to brook no opposition.

At their hesitation, Dorothy looked up in surprise. "Didn't you like the movie?" she asked.

"We didn't go," Bill answered before lapsing into troubled silence. He gave Shirley a slight shove forward.

"Mama—" She hesitated. Then she quickly extended her left hand, where the small stone sparkled. "We're engaged."

Silence. They stood awaiting her verdict. The hall clock hummed ever so lightly.

Dorothy examined the ring, her hand to her mouth. It wasn't exactly unexpected, she thought. After all, they had gone together a long time. But they were so *young!* Shirley was only fifteen, and Bill only nineteen. Yet, he was a solid youth, *intact.* He stood for good things. But Shirley didn't even know any other boys. Maybe they'd forget about it if she could persuade them to wait. Dorothy glanced at Shirley, whose directive look was turned on full blast. And Bill had that chin-out glare that Grandma Casper would have spotted at once. Dorothy reconsidered. After all, she knew she could trust Bill. "Well, all right," she assented.

Two great sighs of relief sounded.

"But you have to promise me one thing," she said.

Eagerly both agreed. The sparkling glow had returned to Shirley's eyes, and Bill's broad grin had replaced his moodiness.

"You've got to promise to wait until Shirley finishes high school."

"Oh, we will, Mama," Shirley cried, throwing her arms around her mother's neck and kissing her. "We will for sure."

"Watch this action!" Bill shouted, his tension exploding.

That fall Bill went to Notre Dame and Shirley entered her junior year. Separation is tragedy for those in love. And it was all of this for Shirley and Bill. In addition, Bill hated the fact that he couldn't play golf in Indiana during the winter. He was used to playing daily. And it struck him as ironic that he was

at Notre Dame on a golf scholarship. In writing of this time in
his life, the columnists have stated that he left the university
because of the "rigors of winter." Well, that's true, in a
fashion. Actually, he didn't mind the snow, the cold, the
ordinary adversities of winter. But he did object strongly to
not being able to play golf. It is this particular "rigor" of
winter that made him leave Notre Dame at the end of the first
semester. But we should also acknowledge that he was separated from his fiancée.

So Billy returned to San Diego and enlisted in the navy,
Shirley was finishing her junior year of high school. But even
though they were reunited, all was not to be smooth for the
lovers. Billy was happy in his station, and he coached some navy
golf teams and helped lay out several courses. But that June,
Shirley's mother had to follow the ship again, this time to the
Bay Area. So once more the two youngsters were separated.
Dorothy held in her heart that perhaps time would add wisdom to their decision. It wasn't that she didn't want Shirley to
marry Bill. She just didn't want Shirley to marry. Not yet.

Thus in the fall of 1951, Shirley came down from the Bay
Area to finish high school at Chula Vista. There had been
many separations, and many hardships. And throughout it all
they had chafed under the strictures. But at last they were on
the back nine. The eighteenth green was in sight. Shirley
would graduate in June.

But Fate has a way of blocking things. The course of true
love could never be satin-smooth. And as June neared, Bill
became moody and irritable. Frustrated in his normal desire to
have his love, he turned silent, resentful. The family friends
with whom Shirley boarded became disturbed and wrote
Dorothy. Others, who perhaps suffered a tinge of envy, whispered bits of gossip, baseless and cruel. This whirling smoke-
storm reached Dorothy, so she talked to Bill and Shirley,
separately, and dismissed the whispers as scurrilous empties.
She smoothed out Bill's resentment.

On the high-school faculty that year was a beloved teacher,

Mrs. Thode. The children affectionately called her "Theodocia," but not to her face. Worried, Dorothy told Theodocia of her troubles. Should Shirley marry Bill?

Mrs. Thode smiled, and the warmth of it was like soft rain falling from an evening sky. "If it's Billy Casper, my dear, it's all right."

The end of school approached, and with it the end of the lovers' restraint. As Shirley says, "We kept our promise—for sixteen days."

Sixteen days after school was out, on June 28, 1952, Shirley and Bill were married by Chaplain John Shilling in the chapel at the Naval Station. Don Chase was best man.

It is interesting to note how the series of houses that Bill has lived in parallel his growth. His earliest boyhood, the New Mexico farmhouse of his Grandpa, provided him with an emotional haven. After his parents separated, he lived for a while with his father, then with his mother. But these were transient situations. Then he started his own home, and the couple lived in a small apartment. Bill's work made him happy, and his home was heaven. How many men can say the same? Concerning his duty, he likes to say, "During the war I made several crossings—on the Coronado ferry." Of his first home— it is too sacred for talk. Bill has always leaned toward silence when anything touches him closely.

Because of a change of station, they had to give up the apartment and move into a secondhand trailer just 16 feet long. When they began touring, they bought a 28-foot trailer with every modern convenience, even to a garbage disposal. Then, as he matured in skill, they purchased a house made up of 930 square feet, a dollhouse that would fit into their present living room. Their next house, a 3,000-square-footer, was on Crela Street in Bonita. Here they planted fruit trees. From this they moved to their present spacious house. Young Billy promptly named it "Spanish Hill," and the name has stuck.

Their first child was born while they lived in the trailer. Linda Maree was to prove the catalyst to bring out Bill's

acceptance of the family. Dorothy had always been to him
"your mother," or formally "Mrs. Rader." He couldn't bring
himself to say "Mother," and "Dorothy" would have shocked
him. So she remained nameless.

After the wedding, Dorothy had returned to the Bay Area.
The young husband was most possessive of his bride and re-
sented any intrusion. After the years of searching for love, Bill
was not about to share the jewel he had found, so Dorothy
stayed away. She understood that Bill had no past experience
by which to gauge the strong love that existed between his
wife and his mother-in-law. But it irked Dorothy to be shut
out. Family affection was the core of life to her, and she
worried while Shirley was pregnant. Was her daughter all
right? Was she working too hard? Lifting things she
shouldn't? And through them all ran the thread of a complaint: She had no family name. No term of affection set
apart just for her. If only Bill would call her something, *anything*, her banishment would be over. With a term of endear-
ment for her, the family would be reunited and love would
flow in its rich, normal channel.

Then on August 11, 1954, Dorothy's phone rang and a
distraught male voice came over the wire. "Shirley's gone to
the hospital," Bill said.

Still no name for her, thought Dorothy. She was still outside the charmed circle. But he *had* called, and he needed
reassurance. "She'll be all right, Bill," Dorothy said. "Shirley's
all right."

"Yeah," Bill answered doubtfully. "I guess so."

He called three times that day. Worried, troubled. And
Dorothy wondered if their taut budget could withstand the
tariff. Then came the fourth call.

"Labor's stopped," Bill announced, pretending diffidence.
"What's it mean?"

Panic reached for Dorothy, but she quelled it. "I don't
know, Bill, but trust in God. Shirley will be all right."

She began to pack, sure she would be needed. Bill would

have to ask her. If he'd just acknowledge his need, he'd be sure to find a name. Why didn't he just say "Mom"? Or "Mother Rader"? Well, at any rate, she'd be ready when he called.

Again the phone rang. "It's a girl!" shouted Bill. "Linda Maree. And Shirley's okay."

A flood of relief passed over Dorothy. In her joy she forgot all about her lack of name. "Oh, Bill, that's wonderful! I'll be right down to help."

"Yeah!" Bill sang out happily. "You do that."

"I'll be on the next train," Dorothy promised.

Never did wheels turn so slowly. Never had there been so many small, useless way stations. But at last the train pulled in.

Bill was waiting. Still shy, still with no name for her, he greeted her eagerly, and his warm, gentle smile told her more than a casual glance. He took her suitcase and they moved out toward the parking area.

Dorothy did the talking, chattering about her long, tantalizing trip. Finally, she touched on the subject nearest to both. "Is your trailer still in Imperial Beach?" Without waiting for an answer, she hurried on. "Can we all fit into it? Soon's we reach it, I'll start getting things ready for when Shirley and the baby come home. Oh—do you have a bottle-sterilizer?"

"The diaper service started today," Bill said.

They came to the car and Dorothy stopped short, turning to Bill in surprise, for the front seat was already occupied by two young ladies.

"I thought they might as well ride along," he said a bit nervously. "You see, Linda's been crying ever since we got home from the hospital. I don't know why. And Shirley was scared."

And so was he.

"We gave her some milk. And we had to change her pants six times. But you know, soon's we got in the car she stopped crying. Funny thing."

Shirley moved over and they got in the car, and for a moment nobody spoke a word. Shirley held out the baby to her mother, who hesitated to take her so brand-new first grandchild.

At last Bill broke the silence and the tension, solving the no-name problem. "Aw c'mon, Granny," he said softly, tenderly.

"She's so *little*," Granny said, her voice tremulous.

"She really won't break, Mama," Shirley reassured.

And Bill said, "Watch this action!"

And they were on their way to the little trailer home on the edge of Imperial Beach.

FOUR
PUTTING IN THE DARK

Into the making of Billy Casper flowed five great streams of influence, five character sources, the elements that make the man: inherent coordination, intactness, love, the health program, and his religion. The last two were yet to come.

The love that entered Bill's life embraced his wife, eventually their children, and his mother-in-law. Though he never called her that. To him the term was opprobrious. It seemed to demean the woman who monitored the Casper family through their early years and into the adult state of togetherness they now hold. No, he never used the term "mother-in-law." Once, when he introduced his family over TV, he referred to Dorothy as "my wife's mother." "Granny" is not a title. It is a name. A name of affection, respect, and love. And she wears it proudly. She is no stock grandmother, but a young and beautiful woman, youthful in mind and body.

33

Intactness, love, and an inherent natural ability to play golf. The long drive he made years ago on the New Mexico farm was but a harbinger of longer drives to come. And most certainly a harbinger of putts. For Billy holds a secure place among golfdom's greats as a putter. He always could putt. But with touring, the rest of his game soon caught up with his ability on the green and the complete golfer emerged.

In his high-school days, Billy further developed his Grandpa's early observation—coordination. He had it inherently, but he increased it into a factor of great importance. His physician-friend, Dr. Charles Franklin, says that Billy has the "greatest eye-to-hand coordination I have ever seen." From that day in the cow-pasture when the boy one-putted the ground squirrel with a rock, this coordination grew and grew until now it is a marvel that Billy's peers view with awe. In virtually every tournament he plays in, Billy produces a putt or two that leaves his gallery gasping.

This is no accident.

In high school he was captain of the golf team. As pointed out, he won the Southern California Interscholastic Championship. He played as often as he could. To do this he had to caddy at the San Diego Country Club. His first job as a caddy came when he was eleven. A year too young. He met his golfer—a lady—at the second hole, and left her after the eighteenth so no one would see him. He says, "I caddied to earn enough money to carry me over the weekend." But the pull of the country club was more than that. The pro, Heaney, immediately spotted Billy's natural ability. Heaney saw that Billy used a "baseball grip" in hitting the ball. And he coached the boy to change to the Vardon grip, which Billy still uses today. Heaney said of Billy, "He's a fine boy, with a natural ability. But he's too lazy." And he gave Billy permission to play on the club course as often as he wished. This meant free golf at a time when Billy would have been hard-pressed to pay. It is interesting to note that his lowest score before changing his grip was a 69. And the first-round total after the grip change was 66.

Most of Billy's putting skill comes from long hours of practice—*in the dark!* His mother moved to the Los Angeles area, and Billy was living in Chula Vista with the Peacocks. Their home was just opposite the fourteenth hole of the country-club course. Jack Peacock, his close friend, says that, often, when the dinner hour approached, his mother would ask him to call Billy. Jack would go out on his front porch, knowing where his classmate could be found.

Across the street, barely visible in the twilight, two boys were putting in the semidarkness. When Jack approached the green, he saw a strange sight. Don Chase, the third of the trio of friends, was on his knees by the hole. He struck a match, stuck it base down in the green on the opposite side of the cup from Billy, who stood, putter in hand, addressing his ball. The match burned for a few seconds, maybe eight or ten. It was enough. Billy spotted the position of the cup, then returned to his ball. The match position in his mind, he never looked at it again. He *knew* where it was. And knowing that, he knew where the hole was. Slowly, with extreme care and equal precision, he drew his club back. By this time the match had gone out, and after its tiny flickering flame, the darkness seemed intensified. Billy hit, and a solid *chock* told of club-head meeting sphere. For a few seconds no one spoke.

Then Don lit another match and held it above the cup. "It's in," he announced. "Man, you don't have to *see* them. You *feel* them in."

And this was precisely the wording others were to use later. Dr. Franklin says, "Casper feels the ball in." Harold Weissman, a sportswriter, said, "Billy putts from memory—from when he practiced after dark." When Billy loses the feel of his putter he's in real trouble. Don Chase says, "It seemed to us, as we donated our dollars to him, that Bill could sink putts whether the sun was out or in moonlight, matchlight, or candlelight. In fact, many a hole was played in complete darkness. Bill could ease up and hit the ball straight whenever he wanted to. The darkness only seemed to add a challenge to the game."

Hundreds of balls rolled across the fourteenth green into the cup during Billy's high-school years. The putting green is practically the only place on which he will practice. And the night-blanketed hours, the numerous *feelings* of the cup-placement and the roll of the green—these are the sources of Billy's phenomenal putting.

Life did not always flow so smoothly for Billy Casper. The biographer's task is to present the whole, not just the favorable parts. Thus it is pertinent to note that in his high-school days, Billy had a profound temper. Today, watching him move calmly on the course, a spectator would never suspect this. But Don Chase says, "Bill's temper in high school would have made Tommy Bolt grab his crinolines and head for cover."

Shades of a broken shaft!

The sessions at the San Diego Country Club did not always end in the dark. Occasionally, the trio of boys would finish with an hour or so of sunlight left. When this happened, they usually went down to Chub's Pool Hall. Chula Vista was a village then. The old and lofty library on F Street stood a block or so from Chub's. Billy and his friends loved to play pool, were good at it. It was fine exercise for the hands and combined accuracy with skill. One evening they finished early and decided they would go to the Pool Hall. But they didn't just *go* there. Being golfers, they *played* their way down—a little over three miles. They played through the town, across streets, around stores and buildings, on toward their eighteenth hole—a spittoon! Don Chase says, "About two or three hours later we approached the library. Bill refused to be stymied."

He took out his pitching wedge and said, "Watch this action."

He swatted the ball a mighty whack and it sailed right over

the gray library—and eventually into Mr. Chub's brass spittoon two blocks away.

Even then he knew that he would become a top golfer. He didn't put it that way, but he has always been psychic, intensely so. He often knows he is going to win a tournament. In Phoenix, 1957, he knew for two days he'd win. This is more than just the confidence a skilled man has in his own production. With Billy, it is a true psychic knowing. And in his schooldays, this quality took the form of protecting his hands. He never explains how he knew. But both his friends, Don Chase and Jack Peacock, recall that he would never join them in any form of football.

"I gotta save my hands," he'd say. And that was his only explanation.

But he did take part in other sports. Don Chase states, "Bill was the best baseball hitter in class. The kids all backed up to the wall when he was at the plate. Bill played varsity baseball, a good game of basketball, and was active in the Hi-Y."

In a highly interesting, relevant letter, Mr. Chase goes on:

Bill was very popular in school. He was never in trouble. He was not the studious type and would not have been even if he had the time—yet his grades, I believe, were above average. Bill's leadership capabilities were evident when the Senior Album showed him as one of two men and five women predicted to be leaders of tomorrow.

Bill's temper was a visible one in those early high-school years. . . . Random boulders, tee-markers, trees, comfort stations, and drinking fountains sometimes felt the chill of cold steel around them on a missed shot. This might be expected. There was a considerable amount of club-throwing at the San Diego Country Club by some of the members during those days, and the kids and caddies emulated this way of expressing displeasure.

Bill soon controlled this, as he had to, in order to become the golfing machine he is now. And he slowed his game down, keeping in the fairways on drives, enabling his fine iron and putting game to work for his sub-par rounds.

Concerning Billy's game in those days, Mr. Chase helpfully points out:

Bill had good concentration on the course, but not nearly as good as he has now. He did not prefer to have close friends follow him at his side down the fairways in tournaments, as he couldn't plan his game and carry on a conversation at the same time.

Bill had what could best be termed an "overly aggressive game." He had an abbreviated backswing, a slight lifting of the right foot while in the backswing, but a tremendously powerful result—300-yard drives were not uncommon. The trouble was, many 300-yard drives were in deep woods or elephant grass. This is where Bill became one of the game's best trouble-shooters, as he played the ball consistently on the green or apron from a tough lie. He taught me and others a lot of the finesse around the greens which he had mastered: the five- or six-iron run-shot on the apron, the soft-slap in a sandtrap, as effortlessly as being on the turf, and the wedge punch-shot for spin.

The writer acknowledges his indebtedness to Don Chase for these most interesting comments. As noted earlier, Don was best man at Bill's wedding, as Bill had been at Don's wedding earlier. And Liz Chase says that she and Shirley have been golf widows since fourteen.

In his navy days, Billy met and played with several men whose names are well known in golf. Gene Littler became a good friend, not alone because he came from the San Diego area (La Jolla), but because they were thrown together on tour. A good-natured rivalry sprang up between them. Another navy golfer who made a mark in professional golf circles was Bud Holscher. And lastly there was Don Collett, perhaps Billy's closest friend. This young man of the Mormon faith helped Billy face several important issues. One was the decision to turn pro. Casper had another mouth to feed now— Linda Maree. And Collett led Billy to his backers.

In April, 1954, Billy applied for membership to the PGA through the Southern California section. Regulations provided that he had to serve an apprenticeship. After the PGA accepted him, he was a member with Approved Player status for five years. At that time he became a Class A member, making him eligible for the Ryder Cup Matches. He could then play as many or as few tournaments as he wished during the year. An Approved Player, to maintain status, must play twenty-five tournaments a year.

When Tom Cushman, the secretary of the County PGA, heard that Billy was about to join his organization, he said, "We'll be happy to have Billy with us. He's the type of guy who will make a fine professional—the teaching variety as well as the one who can win money in PGA tournaments *once in a while*." (The italics are the author's.)

Bob Hummel, of the San Diego Country Club, said, "Bill has a fine temperament for tournament golf. Free and cool. Not easily upset. A natural golfer."

Billy said of himself, "I'd like to make a comfortable living out of golf, and I feel sure I can."

Earl Keller, of the San Diego *Tribune*, commented, "Casper might not ever reach the heights another San Diegan, Gene Littler, has and will in years to come. But Billy is a determined lad, and it will be hard to stop a young man with such a big heart."

One of the most important statements Billy ever made, one that he was to repeat on many occasions, was made originally at this time: "It's a desire you have. That's all it is."

Billy thinks backers are necessary for all amateurs trying to make the shift to the professional ranks. On a three-year contract, Billy's two backers provided him with money, a new car, and a new trailer (the 28-foot job mentioned earlier). Thus Bill and Shirley started tour life, taking Linda Maree along with them.

The life of a professional golfer's wife may seem romantic and exciting to some. And it has its thrilling moments. But there are moments of heartbreak and the stiff upper lip. With a very special job for the woman who would help her man on tour. Early in her experience, Shirley heeded the advice of the wife of another golf pro: "If your husband is having a bad day, imagine how it hurts him, then understand you must be especially strong—for both of you."

For the first few years of their married life, the Caspers' home was anywhere they parked their trailer. They chose a trailer for convenience, comfort, and economy; and also because it was the only way they could be together while Billy played golf. They had a living room with a modern couch, a television, and air-conditioning. The kitchen had a sink with garbage disposal, an apartment-sized stove, and an 8-foot refrigerator. Above these were built-in cabinets that had to be taped shut while traveling so that the contents wouldn't spill out. Between the kitchen and bedroom was a small but compact bath. In the bedroom were twin beds and a small collapsible bed for the baby. And their plans included accommodations for a larger family. They would convert the bedroom into a nursery with built-in bunks and playpen, and would add a sofa-bed for themselves in the living room.

Though they had many comforts, trailer life also presented them with many problems. Shirley said, "Buying groceries is a technique you have to learn. There must be enough food for one stop, but nothing left over to ride to the next town while the refrigerator is disconnected. Sometimes we can't find convenient trailer facilities and must spend the night without water or lights. Sometimes when we are on the road, we find there are feeding problems for Linda. The real strain comes from having to wear a smile, good round or bad, when Daddy comes home."

Shirley's profound influence on Bill's life cannot be too strongly stressed. Her stalwart love, her tremendous faith in him have helped make Bill the man he is. It has not been an easy life. The constant strain, the constant traveling, would wear down anyone less energetic. Concerning her life on tour, Shirley often says, "You learn to live with it, but you never get used to it."

Bill likes his family around him (shades of Grandpa). Being with them each night relaxes him. Pictures of the family show that they reveled in their life. Shirley took care of her baby daughter, their family dog, Pipper, and her man. And this part of her life was the same as those of her village-locked counterparts: keeping her husband happy, which meant keeping him productive. Their neighbors usually were other golfers and their families. The women babysat for each other, shared barbecues and picnics, and ran in and out of each other's trailers for a cup of sugar. On Sundays, Shirley would take Linda Maree to church. And every afternoon Billy played, they waited for him at the clubhouse. But lest the reader feel this is all joy and no labor, let him just think of pulling up roots, of shifting his home, of moving all the gear and furniture of his life, not once—*but forty-five times in a year!*

Billy's first effort toward the U.S. Open in 1955 ended sadly. He did not qualify. (He was to win it just four years later.) Afterward, he went on to San Francisco to see Granny graduate from City College. Then he left for the Western Open, held that year in Portland, where he won his first professional money—all of $33.33. He tied for thirtieth place. During the next few years he was to win the Portland Open three times, a long drive from his initial $33.33.

His first summer tour netted him a little over $3,400, with his best money effort being sixth in the LaBatt Open, with $1,100. The winter tour to follow brought him $3,807, ranking him fifteenth on the PGA list. He was out of the money in only two tournaments that winter. But he was not yet of Masters caliber.

Billy's first big win was the LaBatt Open in 1956. Already that year he had amassed $10,000 but had never had a top spot. On opening day twenty players broke par with Stranahan, the Canadian Amateur Champion (a championship won on the same course), leading with a 67. Billy tied with Leonard and Kroll for a 68. On the second round, Billy's second 68 led the field by one stroke. The third day it rained, but Billy is not a fair-weather golfer, and it didn't bother him. He totaled 203, a lead of three strokes. The final day a strong wind came up, and it looked as if the new young hopeful might wobble under the double pressure of the pack and the weather. He nearly did. On the dog-leg seventieth hole, leading by two, he hooked deep under some pine trees. Hitting one of those low boughs could have spelled a double bogey. But he played his second shot under the branches and brought the ball to a standstill just over the green. Then he chipped his third and one-putted for a par. On the last two holes his calmness returned, and he went on to win like a champion at 274. His first win on the pro circuit: $5,000. Later that day, his golfer friends and their wives slipped into the Casper trailer and decorated it for a party. When Shirley and Bill came home, they were surprised to see a big cake with one candle on it!

We have witnessed three of the five sources of Billy's character: his early intactness, his love for wife and family, and his inherent ability at golf. It is now time to show the genesis of the fourth stream: a health problem. Even as a boy he was overweight. No one thought anything of it. Hadn't Grandpa also been huge? And Billy Earl was like him. Perhaps the tendency to obesity was inherited. But more it was due to a chemical imbalance. Certain foods did not agree with him. And ingestion of these foods caused difficulties, one of which was obesity. Also, we have the word of his best boyhood friend, Don Chase, that Bill possessed a terrible temper, a temper that early in his career he sublimated by moods. Heaney, who changed his grip, called Billy lazy. But the symptoms for laziness are the same as those of fatigue.

He was twenty-four when he won at LaBatt, and he weighed 210. At that time he announced, "I'm going back to San Diego and lose 20 pounds." But he did not lose them.

One other indication of the coming health problem was his dislike of practice. Early in his professional career he found that he tired easily on a driving range, so he stopped practicing.

He said, "If I don't have it when I step out on the course, I won't find it there." He warmed up on the putting green, and on tour got his practice from his rounds. This was a period of apprenticeship, albeit a successful apprenticeship monetarily. In 1957, for Billy Casper, playing golf for a living meant forty to fifty tournaments a year and driving up to 50,000 miles to get to them. And missing a 2-foot putt could mean several thousand dollars. Billy paid off his backers, and they coasted on profit the remainder of their contract. With each success came an added notch of maturation. These were evident in his comments on his game, some sage, some philosophical. He once said, "A cool head and relaxed mental attitude are the most important assets to a successful golfer. Good golf is 70 percent mental confidence and 30 percent mechanics, the physical ability." And: "When you play golf you have to learn to shut the gallery out. And don't give up over a bad round. Get over it as best you can. There's always tomorrow." Also: "A wonderful frame of mind is a main factor of winning." Once more: "You have to learn not to get too elated over good shots and good rounds, nor too depressed over bad placements."

This is Billy's way of saying: Avoid extreme reactions. He is not a talkative man. Challenge, desire, and positive thinking are important for him. And his often-repeated theme is: "It's a desire you have. That's all it is."

The chunky champion carried 200-plus pounds on his Tweedledee-Tweedledum figure. But even then his earnings showed his ability. After ranking twelfth as a moneymaker in 1956, in 1957, he was ninth with $20,807.83, and in 1958 second with $41,323.75.

In November 1957, Jay Hebert, a fellow-golfer, told Don Collett that Casper would become one of golf's all-time greats. Hebert and Billy were playing an exhibition match for TV at Palm Springs. And at first Hebert had thought Billy should go home and learn how to grasp the club. But after Billy fired a 64, beating Hebert by seven strokes, the latter changed his mind.

At the Bing Crosby Tournament in 1956, Billy met a man who was to have a profound influence in his life, Bob Reynolds, a former All-American Stanford tackle and president of the California Angels. For years Bob has participated in Billy's important decisions, either personally or by wire or letter.

Early in 1957 the Caspers sold their trailer and began living in motels. For three years the trailer had been home and hearth, but they had outgrown it. Their second child, young Billy, had arrived on November 2, 1956. And as the family grew, so did Billy's skill. His win at LaBatt entitled him for the first time to play in the Tournament of Champions, at Las Vegas. He came in second, a spot he has held several times. He has never won it. Granny laughingly refers to him as the Tournament of Champions bridesmaid.

Another important tournament that year was the Masters, in Augusta, Georgia—that he received an invitation after so brief a career was an honor. In it he tied with five others, among them Byron Nelson, at sixteenth spot, for $778.75.

In April, flying to the Kentucky Derby Tournament, he caught a cold. Colds began to occur more frequently, and with them a troublesome sinus condition. But even so, Billy won the tournament.

An amusing incident that demonstrated a warm side to Billy's character occurred in Philadelphia in the summer of 1957. A group sat on the terrace of the club, among them Julius Boros and his wife, and Alice and Ken Everett, close friends of the Caspers. Billy had finished and joined the group. Two small boys came running for autographs. Billy signed their books and the pair left.

"Oh, boy!" exclaimed one. "Sam Snead!"

"Why did you do that, Bill?" asked Alice.

Bill grinned broadly. "He doesn't know who I am, so that'll make him happy."

Somewhere in America today is a young man who will not know until he reads this that his prized autograph of Snead is actually a prized autograph of another great golfer—Billy Casper.

The Crosby in 1958 was a $50,000 event at Pebble Beach, California. On the last round, Billy was tied with Rosburg at 206. They played in the same foursome, so it was really a confrontation match. Asked later if this worried him, Billy replied, "Never. I went out to try for pars. I never felt it was head-to-head play. There were other fellows close to us in scores, if I wanted to worry." Before the tee-off that day, Billy said to himself, "I'll just go out and play, that's all. Just play. You can't worry about who's ahead or behind you and be able to play your own game." The real strength of his game has always been his concentration. He allows nothing to disturb him. His eyes are only for the ball and the pin on the green. Once he was asked if he'd noticed that his gallery was larger than usual that day. He replied, "I never see them." He never worries about the last shot, or the next. He advises, "Hit one shot at a time. Don't game needlessly. Play it safe for pars and hope for birdies." A newspaperman, Art Rosenbaum, said, "Casper is casual about everything. He seems to accept an eagle two with the same aplomb as a splash in the sandtrap."

At the Crosby, Billy played all four rounds under par to win at 277, four strokes ahead of the number-two man, Dave Marr. On the eleventh hole, he used a nine-iron to belt the ball 135 yards. It bounced twice and finally dropped in, an eagle two. In spite of this, on the sixteenth hole he felt he needed to talk to himself. What did he say? "Bill, there's nothing to worry about. Keep playing and start swinging a little more." Billy's top money was $4,000. With his partner and close friend, amateur Bob Reynolds, he picked up second-place best-ball total of 261 and an additional $1,500.

After the Crosby, Billy came down with another cold and developed a severe backache. Also, his sinus bothered him

46 BILLY CASPER: WINNER

greatly. But in March, at New Orleans, he played Ken Venturi to a 72-hole tie, resulting in a sudden-death playoff. Rain had plagued the affair, and though Venturi and Casper were slated for an eighteen-hole round, the storm changed their plans to the sudden-death. Both parred the 393-yard number one in four. On the 477-yard par-five second hole, Billy was on the green in two. Venturi's second went into the sand, but he blasted out to lie only 2 feet from the pin, all set up for a birdie. Billy addressed his ball, and as always hit at once. The ball rolled and rolled, and at last plopped in for an eagle three, winning the tournament and $2,800. The San Diego *Evening Tribune* that night carried what must be almost the only picture of Billy clowning, acting out Grandpa's definition of his name, "the cut-up." The shot shows Billy with a towel wrapped maharaja-style around his head and kissing his putter. Even the great, the conservative, serious great, sometimes take a day off.

At the Tournament of Champions in Las Vegas, Billy led during the first three days. On the final day, at the seventeenth hole, tension was tremendous. Billy was tied with Canadian Stan Leonard. But on the seventeenth, using a two-iron, Billy's shot strayed to the right into a lagoon. He took his penalty and dropped his ball, and promptly hooked this one in another lagoon. Leonard finished with a tournament record of 275, and Billy followed by one shot, 276. A shot that was the difference between Leonard's $10,000 and the $5,000 Billy took home.

By this time, Granny had returned to the area. The Caspers had recently bought a small tract home on Corte Maria. Bill needed Shirley with him on tour, so Granny took over the care of the Casper children while their parents were away. This was a happy arrangement, because by now Granny had her second family of two: John, aged three, and Margee, a baby.

In June 1958, Billy won the Buick Open, at Grand Blanc, Michigan, the day before his twenty-seventh birthday. A

severe thunderstorm chased the pros off the course on the
last day. Griping sounded throughout the clubhouse as orders
came to go back out. This was one of the big-money events
of the year—first prize of $9,000. Only one player was smil-
ing. Billy sat on the floor, back against a locker, and said,
"Either we play it or we don't. Why get excited about it?"
He won the $9,000.

Jack Murphy said:

Billy's idea of an attractive tournament is one that gets him off
the tee early in the morning, leaving time for some trout fishing
before sunset. . . . If there's such a thing as a perfect temperament
in golf, it belongs to Casper. It would be an exaggeration to say
that nothing ruffles him. Only a moron could have that experience, and Casper is a man of high intelligence. Casper's strength
is that he refuses to indulge himself in petty tantrums. He masters
his emotions and accepts adversity with grace. And, equally
important, he wears his success with the same style.

By now Billy had shifted his hook into a fade. As he said,
"Though I was able to finish in the money with a hook, it
soon became apparent to me that I would be able to do better
if I could achieve a left-to-right flight on the ball. I would
wind up in less trouble. . . . The principal thing a golfer must
do to eliminate a hook is to get the left hip out of the way on
the downswing and especially at impact." This change from
a hook to a fade was actually a change in his whole game. He
accomplished it in less than six months, and he analyzed his
problem and corrected it himself, with no assistance. He
moved the ball farther up off his left toe, making the club-
head come from outside the ball. It is the most significant
change he has ever made in his game.

Billy came in second to Finsterwald in the PGA, played
that year it Haverstown, Pennsylvania. At Gleneagles, in
Chicago, two weeks later Billy shot a weird 80, 64, 64, 67—
275. After the first day's horrible catastrophe, the two 64's
and the 67 brought him back to finish a respectable seventh.
He was only three strokes behind the winner. It is worth

noting that these two 64's are course records. He finished the year as second top money-winner with $41,323.75

But early in 1959 things began to change. Even a good golfer can have a bad streak. By the time the Tournament of Champions came along in April, Billy was in a slump. "I suppose it had to happen," he said philosophically. "Sooner or later everybody has to suffer in this game. Gene Littler had to battle out of a long slump. So did Mike Souchak and Cary Middlecoff. Naturally I don't like it. I don't understand it. But I don't intend to let this thing get the best of me. When I come out of it, I think the experience will have made me a better player."

He was scowling, though, when he missed five short putts in eleven holes in the second round of the Tournament of Champions.

"That's the way it's going this year," he said resignedly. "I'm playing about as well as ever, but I can't score. Last year I made a lot of those 4- and 5-foot putts. But they won't go in for me now."

Though Billy was in a slump, he was still a happy player, and the gallery loved to follow him. During the Tournament of Champions he was playing a shot out of the deep rough when he noticed the marshals pushing back the gallery.

"It's all right," he said, grinning. "Go easy on the people. They have just as much right to be in the rough as I have."

Bill's cycle of winning began to reverse itself. By April 1959, he had not won a single tournament. And his biggest score came in the San Diego Open in late January when he collected $1,320 for finishing in a five-way tie for second. He came home from tour with a bad back. Things looked bleak. And the U.S. Open was coming in June at Mamaroneck, N.Y. The Open, the golfer's crown. Feeling low, in a slump, Billy returned to the tour and Mamaroneck. He was a young man with positive determination, a great heart, yet with mounting weight and health problems, and his colorful personality had gone into retreat.

Even the weather got into the act. On Thursday a steady mist drenched the early starters. On Friday brisk gusts of wind up to 25 miles an hour snatched at drives and pitches alike, sending the balls in eccentric arcs. Saturday two floods forced postponement of play for an hour and fifty minutes in the morning and an hour and a half in the afternoon. Temperatures were in the 50's, calling out sweaters and rainsuits for warmth. Because of the typhoonlike rains and the strong winds, for the first time the contestants played eighteen holes on Sunday instead of the customary grueling 36 on Saturday. Only once in the history of the Open, which dates back to 1895, has the event been postponed. In 1901 the assassination of President McKinley caused a one-week delay. Walter Travis scored a second-straight victory that year. The Open had had bad weather before, such as in Fort Worth in 1941, or Toledo in 1957. But never for the entire route.

On Wednesday, Billy decided to go against one of his profoundest beliefs. He practiced for an hour and a half. Whether that caused it, or whether Lady Luck decided to return her smile after the winter of frowning, no one knows. Or it may have been just good omens. He was number 59, it was the 59th U.S. Open, and his caddy wore number 59. At any rate, at the end of the second day's play, Billy led the pack by one stroke, 139. He'd had 28 putts the first round, and thirty the second. He was thrilled at leading going into the third day. That third round, he used only 27 putts for a 69, so that on the last day he led by three. Behind him were some of golf's greats: Hogan at 211, Rosburg, Palmer, and Harmon, the local pro, at 212, and Souchak at 213. Billy never lost the lead. On the fourth, a bee stung him on the chest. Lionel Hebert was putting, and Billy spent a few anguished moments holding his sweater and shirt, trying to confine the insect without making a fuss. Finally he was able to drop the bee on the green. The sting hurt for several hours.

Rosburg tied Billy on the twelfth, at 258, but took a double-bogey five on the next hole and never got back. On

the fourteenth, Billy made his best shot and the greatest shot
of the tournament with a 12-foot putt that put him three
strokes in the lead. He hit a four-iron for his second shot,
which came down 12 feet to the right of the hole. He knew
he had to sink it. He hadn't had a birdie since the fifth. And
he did have four bogeys. So he made the putt for a birdie 3.
After the fourteenth, he hoped just for pars to hold on. On
the last few holes he hurried, partly because of the wind and
the coming storm, but mainly to put pressure on those behind
him, to make them worry about him. So he bogeyed the
fifteenth and seventeenth. Rosburg matched Casper's par on
the sixteenth with a breathtaking shot—a 40-foot putt that
lipped out. Rosburg parred the seventeenth, which left him
just one stroke back with the final hole to play.

Billy was already in, watching from the club window. If
Rosburg birdied, it was a tie. Billy's voice dropped to a
smoothness that those who knew him would say indicated
worry. But the interviewing reporters were struck with his
calmness. Rosburg made a fine drive. Then his six-iron shot
left him 35 feet short of the pin, and his putt stopped 5 feet
short.

It was Billy's biggest win: 282, $12,000, the biggest purse
in Open history; $4,000 more than Tommy Bolt had won the
previous year. Billy had only 114 putts, exactly thirty under
par on the greens, nine one-putt greens, the last four of the
third round, the first five of the fourth round. On the second
he had a 10-footer, on the sixteenth a 6-footer, on the seventeenth a 15-footer, and on the eighteenth a 3-footer.

The boy was a man, Casper—man of Golf!

FIVE

GOOD-BY TO GOLF

Problems of health began to creep into Billy Casper's game—
backaches, sinus infections, colds, muscle spasms, obesity. His
scores began to show a cyclic swing from zenith to nadir.
The first tournament in 1959 was the Los Angeles Open,
where he tied for twenty-first. A poor score is not by itself
too meaningful, but the erratic drop from good to bad, from
top positions to luckless ties in the twenties—the very irregu-
larity of this is almost a symptom in itself, for steadiness is
the heart of Billy Casper.

At the Tijuana Open, one week after Los Angeles, he was
too ill to show. At the Bing Crosby the next week he tied for
fourteenth, winning $712. Erratically, at the San Diego Open
he tied for second but offset this good showing the following
week by tying for twenty-sixth at Phoenix. At the Greater
New Orleans Open the first two days he shot a 76, 76,

51

thereby failing to qualify. And again at the Masters he failed
to qualify, once more shooting a 76, 76. Before the Open in
June, a strong flu virus caused Billy to miss seven events. The
Open title brought new responsibilities. Sponsors demanded
he play more, which left less time for fishing between tournaments. Billy said, "Golf has been good to me; I'll give back to
it all I can." And so, where a chapter existed, he began to give
seminar-demonstrations to the Junior Golfers. Because of his
new title, Billy decided he must remain on tour longer.

The erratic scoring continued. Two weeks after his Open
win, Billy failed to qualify at Gleneagles and some of the
sportswriters were making innuendoes about his "accidental"
win at Mamaroneck. There was nothing accidental about it.
The putting record alone showed it was not accidental. And
as Billy said, "You can't putt it till you get it there." The
erratic scorings both before and after the Open showed the
cause to be a health problem, not one of skill, or lack of it.

In July he accepted an invitation to the Utah Open at Salt
Lake City. This was not a PGA-sponsored tournament, and
that august body fined Casper $100 for the error. Billy
should have checked, but he didn't, and there was a scheduled
tournament at Hartford that week. The Utah Open marked
a turning point in his life. It also marked the beginning of the
fifth and final element that makes the man that Billy Casper is
today. To Billy it seems almost Fate that every time he has
faced an important decision, some Mormon has stood beside
him to help, even during the years before he joined the Mormon Church. Don Collett, a Mormon, advised him to turn pro
and also arranged for him to meet his original backers.

In Salt Lake City Bill and Shirley were immediately struck
with the importance that the Mormons attach to family life.
They formed friendships that would cast a golden glow over
the rest of their lives. Early they met Ferrell and Theda
Horsley, a couple Granny had known in Washington. Ferrell
had befriended Dorothy during a crisis in her life, and the
couple knew Shirley well. The Horsleys' three children were

stalwart evidence of the love and affection poured over them by wise God-understanding parents. The Caspers also met Barbara and Hack Miller, who was later to officiate at their baptism. A sports editor on the *Deseret News*, Hack has been a guiding hand for their church experience. The Millers have four boys, and they, too, bear staunch evidence of the great value Mormons place on family life. The president of the Utah Golf Association, Steve Dunford, invited Shirley and Bill to his home for a patio dinner. Others who befriended them were Oma and Stan Wagstaff, and Malu Hoopiiaina and his wife. The Hawaiian later became Billy's fishing companion. All of these showed a genuine and sincere friendship for the California couple. But more important, all of these people were splendid examples of the warmth and depth of feeling that hold a Mormon family together, that make family life a sturdy girder in the structure of the Mormon Church. This strength through love made a deep impression on Shirley and Bill.

In August, Billy caught the chicken pox from Linda Maree. He came down with it at Akron, where he shot a 67, 69, 67, 70—273—to tie for seventh place and win $875. He said he was so bushed he didn't know whether the playing was worth it. A penicillin shot gave him a bad reaction, and he left the tour.

In October he won the Portland Open with 69, 64, 67, 69 —269. A short time later he captured the Lafayette and the Mobile, which, with the U.S. Open, made four wins out of five starts.

The next year, 1960, was slim. It opened with an ominous portent. At the Los Angeles Open, Billy tied for thirty-first place! The win was $275, a quiddity for the U.S. Open champion. But the erratic ups and downs of his scoring called for a change, which he accomplished by tying for fourth at San Diego. Again it must be noted that a single low score, or even an erratic scoring on the part of certain golfers, is not too meaningful. But for a man whose consistency, steadiness, and regularity of performance are hallmarks of his character, such paradoxic scoring is indicative of deep trouble. And that trouble was ill health, slowly and insidiously building, evident at this time in obesity, moodiness, frequent colds, headaches, muscular spasms, and general malaise.

After the Tucson, where he tied for sixteenth, Billy left the tour for five weeks. Perhaps fiishing would bring surcease. He came back to San Diego, where his family, fearful of his temperamental moodiness and occasional flare-ups, moved about the house balancing their eggs carefully.

Early in April, Billy went to the Masters. The fishing had done him good, the home life had relaxed his taut muscles, and he came in fourth with a 71, 71, 71, 74—287. The money was $5,250, which looked very good indeed in this slim year.

On April 16, 1960, Billy became a full-fledged Class-A member of the PGA. He'd served his stint as an "approved player." But his record remained poor, his position way down. Poor health was a stone around his neck, maddening poor health in that the doctors could find nothing. And even the symptoms which he himself noted didn't show up consistently. At the Colonial he tied for thirtieth place, and for twenty-fourth at the 500 Festival two weeks later. Remember, these high finishes were those of the U.S. Open champion. No wonder sly digs occurrred in the papers. Billy's career was ebbing.

To add to Casper's worries, his son, Billy, had a sudden attack of a mysterious illness. With no previous upset, one afternoon young Billy developed a fever of 106! Death hovered, and no doctor could find a cause. They rushed the boy to the hospital, hopefully filled him with antibiotics, and prayed. Tests showed nothing. Then just as suddenly the fever abated.

The tour is a hard taskmaster, and sponsors formidable. So the distraught father, himself subject to inexplicable attacks of various aches and pains, remained on tour, anxiety riding high. In June the dreaded malady struck young Billy again, devastating the household. Bill and Shirley were home from the tour, but parental love was insufficient and Billy grew worse. Shirley was pregnant and could not go to the hospital to be with him. So Bill requested Granny to go. She stood solitary watch, helpless and almost hopeless, with prayer the only defense. That defense was sufficient. Again the antibiotics and icepacks brought down the temperature. And a few weeks later the family pediatrician found the cause, a hypo-gamma-globulin anemia. With the administration of maintenance dosages of gamma-globulin—using a frighteningly mammoth needle that horrified the boy and Granny alike—little Billy's gamma-globulin count began its climb back to normal. The doctor warned, however, that for the rest of his life he would have to have scheduled maintenance dosages.

In July, at the PGA, Billy tied for twenty-fourth spot. At the Salt Lake City Open, now a PGA event, and one where he wanted to play his best for his new-found friends, he tied for nineteenth.

The third week of September he went to Portland, the site of his very first money—that $33.33 in 1955. He won the Portland with a 68, 67, 66, 65—266. He was in a fine mood. His game was good, his health apparently on the recovery fairway, and things looked sunny again. He said, "The holes kept getting in the way of my ball." He had also won this tournament the preceding year. With this 1960 win, he became the first professional that year to defend a title successfully.

The cycle was on the up, and the week after the Portland he won the Hesperia Open, and two weeks later the Orange County Open. But whatever goes up eventually comes down, and that's the way Billy's spirits inexplicably went. He left the tour for another five weeks' fishing, and his family gingerly tiptoed about the house. The virtuoso was in residence, taut, angry as a red-hot hornet, demanding four eggs if offered two, or none at all if offered four.

On a warm fall day, Granny came to pay her morning call at the Casper home on Crela Street. Bright-eyed and beauti-

ful, she smiled her way into the house. Her red slacks—and
Granny could wear slacks—made a twinkling highlight in the
morning sun as she entered the patio, where Shirley was snip-
ping roses.

"Good morning, love," Granny said, her voice lilting.

"Good morning, Mama," Shirley answered, smiling widely.

Bill lay sprawled in a lounge chair, his paper over his face.
There was no way to tell whether he was awake or asleep,
except that every curve of his ample body showed resentment.
Resentment of the morning (*Why was everybody so cheer-
ful!*), resentment of the mocking bird's melody (*Damn bird,
making all that fuss!*), resentment of Shirley, of Granny, of
the kids. In fact, resentment of just everybody and everything. He was about ready to roar. They'd better keep their
distance!

Granny moved gracefully across the flagstones, paused by
the recumbent figure, and lifted the newspaper. "Good morning, Bill," she greeted.

Bill bolted erect, glaring. His face turned cold. Startled,
Granny drew back. Bill got to his feet, his mountainous hunk
of flesh aggrieved. He straightened, and it seemed to Granny
he'd never been so tall. Nor so furious. What had she done?
Then, without a word, Bill turned haughtily and stamped
across the patio and into the house. Devastation spread like a
wake behind him. Granny's eyes flashed anger. A highly sensitive woman, she did not well endure rebuke, even if there
were cause for it. And with no cause, it became an insult.

She strode toward the gate. "I'll never speak to him again,"
she vowed. The gate shook the garden wall.

Near noon, Granny's phone rang. "Mama," Shirley hesitated, "I'm awfully sorry. Bill has been in a terrible mood all
week and I just don't know what to do."

"But why?" demanded Granny. "Didn't he win last week?"

"Yes," Shirley agreed. "He won $2,000 at the Orange
County Open. But something's the matter with him. We're all
walking on eggs."

"I'm not going to," Granny stated. "He can't be rude to me. He's your man, not mine."

About three-thirty that afternoon, Granny was raking leaves in her yard when a strange procession came up the front walk. First, all she could see was a bouquet of roses. A large bouquet, with many tiny pink roses. Behind the roses she saw Bill, a smile of half-embarrassment, half-plea for approval shining on his cherubic face. Behind Bill, Shirley hurried along, shaking her head, her lips silently forming the sounds "I didn't say a word, Mama."

Bill stopped, extended the roses, and grinned his most angelic grin. "I'm sorry, Granny," he said softly.

Love welled within Granny. "Oh, Bill," she sobbed, taking him in her arms.

The hornet's stinger had been extracted.

The year 1960 came to a thin close. Buffeted by ailments he could not identify, subject to temperamental tantrums, plagued by backaches and sinus and headaches, Billy ended his sixth year as a professional. Financially he slipped back from the preceding two years, winning $31,060.83. He placed first in three tournaments, the Portland, the Hesperia, and the Orange County opens. Much more important, he won his first Vardon Trophy, one of the highest honors a golfer can attain, consisting of the best average score for sixty rounds. This was later changed to eighty rounds, twenty tournaments.

The year 1961 began with the same vacillating from up to down. In the San Diego Open, he tied for twenty-first. At the Bing Crosby the next week, he set a new course record, whipping Pebble Beach with a seven-under-par 65. He used only 23 putts for the eighteen holes. But due to a nagging headache that depleted the aspirin bottle, even a course record of 65 was insufficient to raise the 75, 73, and 74 he had made in the preceding days. He ended tied for twenty-fifth place. An up-and-down within a tournament.

After the Phoenix Open in February, Billy dropped out of the tour for five weeks. Fishing was the excuse, ill health was the reason. At the Masters, he tied for sixth, winning $3,200. At the Houston, the Tournament of Champions, the Colonial, and the Indianapolis 500 Festival, Billy did become steady again, placing in a tie at from ninth to sixth. Fair enough, but not the distinguished record to be expected from a former U.S. Open champ.

The 1961 U.S. Open was at the Oakland Hills Country Club, in Birmingham, Michigan, and Billy arrived one day later than the other golfers, on Monday. "The yellowtail fishing was hot at home, and I couldn't leave," he explained. On the plane coming in, ever gallant, Billy offered to help a stewardess open a package. He took out his pocketknife and somehow managed to jab it deep into his right hand. On opening day he insisted the wound didn't bother him, but he had trouble with his drive. He was in the rough nine times off the tee. "I've got a sore back from hitting the ball out of the rough," he announced, grinning. "The wind drove me half-crazy. If I allowed for it, it would either change direction or stop blowing. I shot a 74, but it should have been an 85."

He tied for fifteenth with a 290. At the PGA two weeks later he held the same spot, fifteenth, but it took a 286 to do it.

At the Carling, in the middle of August, on the third day, Billy led with a 206. This in spite of a course record-breaking 64 by Ted Kroll. Paul Harney was second with a 208. But that aching back throbbed again, and Billy slipped to a tie for third, with a 279.

The next week at Akron, where rubber fumes blanket the countryside (to the consternation of the Chamber of Commerce), Billy had to withdraw ill after the second day. He was out for five weeks, a peevish, sulky guy, and his family gave him respectful distance.

He came back to win the Portland Open for the third time. Because of these three Portland wins, during the annual tournament today, that city proudly dubs itself "Caspertown." On the last day of the 1961 Portland, Billy started three strokes off the pace set by Hill for the first three rounds. On the twelfth hole, a par five, Billy made a 16-foot putt for an eagle, thereby catching his twenty-four-year-old competitor. Billy went on to win by one stroke with a fifteen-under-par 273.

As the two men strode from the green, Casper said to Hill, "Dave, that's too bad. You played beautifully."

Dave managed a dazed acknowledgment. "I hate to lose," he said to the crowd. "Even if it's to nice people like Casper."

Billy came back, "I think Dave should have won it. But I'm a little older, and maybe he wanted me to get another victory before I retired!"

Shirley joined in, "Both of us were wondering if we were ever going to win any more tournaments."

It was Billy's first, and only, win of the year, though he ranked fourth in earnings.

October found Billy in England on his first Ryder Cup team. The solid gold cup, which the Americans returned to England with them, was lost for a while due to a bit of confusion on the part of Jerry Barber, team captain. But after a few anguished hours it was rescued and the Americans won again. As a parting gift, the British team presented to each American a gaudy green tie, striped with light gold that wore thin red boundaries, a most colorful cravat.

1962 opened with a good portent: Billy hit his second hole-in-one, a 207-yard shot with a five-iron on the eighteenth hole of the Stardust Country Club in San Diego. But in the first seven tournaments he did poorly. In the L.A. Open he tied for thirty-second. At San Diego he tied for fifteenth. At the Bing Crosby he tied for fifty-first place in one of the wettest tournaments on record. At the Lucky International he tied for third, which brought him $2,500, his best money so far that year. At the Palm Springs he tied for thirtieth. For many golfers—for most, actually—such scores would simply rate them as just not up to it ("up to par" would be no pun). But such results are not Casperlike scores. They are the product of general malaise. At Phoenix he tied for second, which brought him $2,300. He then left the tour to replenish his reservoir of intactness by deep-sea fishing. For six weeks the yellowtail calmed his depressed mind.

On March 22 he rejoined the tour at the Doral Open in Miami. On the last day, a blond young rookie, Paul Bondeson, led the pack at two under par with a 34 on the front nine. Casper was three strokes behind as he rounded the turn. Most of golfdom's great stared over their shoulders as the two leaders battled head-to-head in the same foursome. Bondeson wilted under the pressure. The wind howled over the course, wreaking havoc with the last day's scores. Only eight turned in subpar totals. On the last green, Bondeson rimmed the cup with a stunning 10-foot putt that could have netted him a sudden-death playoff. But Billy shot a 71, for a total of 283, five under par, winning by one stroke a prize of $9,000. But actually the winning shot was Billy's 35-foot putt on the fifteenth hole, where Bondeson took a bogey.

At the Masters, amid the sky-blessed pleasures of pink and white dogwood, the beautiful camellias, and the prodigal azaleas, the Caspers and their friends, the Bob Reynoldses, had a bad experience trying to find acceptable lodging. They had paid a $250 deposit on the total premium of $550. They entered the house, stepping gingerly to avoid cockroaches and other evidence of filth. They walked right out again, forfeiting their deposit. Also, Billy was paired with Jerry Barber next to last in the opening round and had to finish in the dark. In another group Gardner Dickinson made his approach shot to the eighteenth and yelled, "Fore to the left." Amateur Charles Coe hit his and cried, "Fore to the right." When Billy hit his, he couldn't see where it went. "Fore anywhere," he whooped. Ordinarily his boyhood experience would have aided him here. But his health problem was intensifying and he acquired a "mental block," finishing eleven shots off the winning 280.

No one ever forgets the Masters. But a slight measure of the sting of unpleasantness was lifted for Billy the next week when he won the Greater Greensboro Open. Again the wind was a terror, and the favorite native son (adopted), Mike Souchak, added to the difficulties. Mike built a four-stroke lead after seven holes of the front nine. He kept the lead at three through the twelfth hole. Then Billy birdied the thirteenth and Mike went one over on the fifteenth. On the sixteenth, Casper's drive went into the ugly creek that cuts all the way across the fairway. But Mike also paddled his canoe in the same creek. Casper dropped his ball and survived with a bogey by sinking a 7-foot putt. It just wasn't Mike's day. After dropping back for a one-stroke penalty, Mike hit his third shot onto the green, and two-putted for his double bogey. Still somewhat shaken, he bogeyed the seventeenth, and what had been a three-stroke lead on the twelfth became a one-stroke loss after the seventeenth. Casper parred the eighteenth. Mike made a spectacular clutch approach shot. It was dead in line, and the gallery stopped breathing. Then the ball slowed, finally came to rest. It lacked the power for just one more turn. That one turn of the ball was worth $1,900 to Billy—the difference between the top money of $5,300 and the $3,400 Souchak took home. Billy had a 69, 70, 68, 68—275, nine under par. Perhaps it didn't recompense for the Masters, but it did bring Casper to $22,608 for the year, second only to Palmer.

At Las Vegas in May, a sore back and muscle spasms were a real distress and Billy lost to Arnold Palmer. This marked the third time Billy took the bridesmaid's position at the tournament reserved for only the winners of other tournaments. Arnold and Billy came even to the final hole. Casper's tee-shot hooked into the rough, giving him a difficult lie that forced him to carry over a tree. Palmer was in the middle of the fairway on the par-four hole. Casper's second shot from the rough soared over the tree but was short of the green by about 25 feet and into the gallery. Palmer's second shot was just off the green in the grass, about 20 feet from the hole.

The gallery hushed, tense, as Billy took a sand wedge from

his bag. If he could chip close to the hole, he could sink his putt for a par and perhaps force Palmer into a playoff.

Billy's chip shot was magnificent. The crowd roared a thunderous approval as the ball rolled across the green and stopped 3 feet from the pin.

But Palmer stroked his long putt into the cup for a birdie, and the show was over. He won with 276, twelve under par. Billy shot a 277—73, 67, 68, 69. That first day, that 73, Casper's ailing back knocked him down. Billy was two under par and on the eighth fairway when the pain flashed over him. His last six holes were one birdie, one par, and four bogeys. Fortunately Dr. Franklin was in the gallery. He suggested steam baths and massage, and Bill responded so well that the next day he carded a 67, low round for the tournament. But even the 67, 68 of his last two days were not enough to overtake Palmer. Once again the Tournament of Champions was an aloof lady. Billy's mounting health problem continued to work its way into his game.

At the Indianapolis 500 Festival Open a few weeks later, Billy won with a 264, *twenty* under par! He needed a birdie on the eighteenth to win, and his magic putter produced the required shot.

The health problem, baffling, nagging, rarely identifiable, pursued Billy relentlessly. On a cyclic pattern, two weeks after his 500 Festival victory, he slipped down to tie for twenty-third in the Thunderbird. And one week after that—whisper the heresy!—Casper failed to qualify for the Open! The Open he'd won three years earlier. Rugged is the life of the touring golfer. The rest of the year his record rose and fell mercurially, from second in the Western Open to tied for fifty-first in the PGA—*fifty-first!* At Akron, the American Golf Classic, once more he failed to qualify. All symptoms were go now, to borrow from astrophysics. And each syndrome held a malignant source of trouble. Up and down, tied for twenty-second at Doral, tenth at Seattle. Then Portland—"Caspertown." Lady Luck relented a little: Billy was third, with 66, 68, 67, 71—272. The final tournament of the year was at Bakersfield. Billy won with a 272, sixteen under par. Healthwise, the year was distressing, but not so financially. Casper finished fourth in the money, with $61,842.19.

Billy started 1963 with a new putting stance, "with a narrow-open rather than a wide-closed stance," as he put it. This was the first major change in his game since he shifted to the fade approach. At San Diego he played the last three days with intestinal flu, finishing in third place. He should have quit, but he refused to leave the course, because he and Littler had been built up as drawing cards. He won the Crosby at Pebble Beach. On the final hole, Billy played it safe off the tee with a two-iron. In the middle of his swing a spectator walked behind him, his shadow falling on the ball. Billy shanked the ball into a trap on the right. Par was far away. The eighteenth is long and oceangoing. He chose his nine-iron, followed with a two-iron. And then made what he considers one of the greatest shots in his career—a 70-foot pitch that rolled within 1 foot of the pin. The gallery stamped and shouted as he plunked in his par.

He and Shirley watched the rest of the tournament on the TV in the press room. It was a series of gaspers, breath-holders, and sighs of relief. First, Player pitched to within 12 feet of the hole to lie three. He needed a birdie to tie, but he couldn't pull the final putt. Then came Duden, who also needed a birdie to tie. Three putts later his threat had vanished. Lastly, the redoubtable Nicklaus came on the screen. He made a beautiful drive. But his approach to the green went wide behind a tree. He pitched brilliantly to make the green in three. A two-putt par would tie him with Billy. He shot past the hole, and had trouble when he came back, and ended with a three. Casper won with 73, 65, 73, 74—285.

Increasing discomfort, constant sleepiness in the morning, headaches, all drove Billy further and further down. His moodiness deepened and he began to gripe at the gallery. He told one interviewer: "Thirty thousand people! That's a lot of people. And I know it isn't easy to control them. But I think the marshals are partly at fault. They won't give orders, aren't vocal enough." This from gentle Billy Casper.

At the Greater Greensboro Open, on the eighth hole of the third round, he had a side-hill lie. His ball was in a divot. He hit the ball and he could feel something snap in the palm of his left hand. This was the beginning of an almost crippling injury. He finished the tournament despite the pain, tying for twentieth place. Later, his hand seemed to calm down and he continued the tour at the Houston Open, where he tied for tenth.

By the time he reached the Tournament of Champions, his hand was shooting with pain. He took heat treatments, and everybody came forward with helpful (?) suggestions. One even suggested he play one-handed. On the final round, the ninth hole, he hit his drive and the pain grabbed him. He screamed. He couldn't close his hand. The pain was agony. The PGA official ordered him to continue his playing. He argued, but finally hit the ball, a quail-high stroke that went into a right trap. Shirley rushed inside the ropes, knowing something was wrong. People were crying, some clapping, some screaming. Others called, "Sorry, Billy." Each hand movement punished the already torn muscles. And so, though he was in second place and a shot ahead of Palmer, he picked up his ball, signifying he had withdrawn. The applause continued for at least five minutes.

The doctors called it tendonitis. They taped it, gave him cortisone. He came home, believing he'd be off the tour for only three weeks. But at the end of ten he still couldn't grip a club. Fishing was a balm to him, though because of his injury he couldn't tackle the mighty marlin. An orthopedic surgeon put his hand in a cast for ten days.

His playing career seemed to be over. Or at least, as he reasoned, it had certainly been shortened. He had already had a career, but his playing time certainly seemed cut off earlier than it should have been. Nothing left but a soft pro job in some club. Indeed, someone did come forward with an offer. And though the initial injury bore no seeming relation to allergy, still the mounting health problem compounded the difficulty. He was moody and irritable. A serious ear infection developed, heightening Billy's troubles. He was way over-weight—225 pounds. And Dr. Klug, an internist and cardiac specialist, told Granny that he was worried about Billy's heart, that he must lose weight or he'd keel over one day. Dr. Klug was also concerned over Billy's high uric-acid level. Obviously Billy had been suffering from gout for a long time. Drs. Franklin and Klug advised a bone specialist for the wrist. The latter prescribed some exercises and some mechanical grips, but these were ineffective. Billy returned to Bonita to sit in pain and despair.

The world was bleak, and golf seemed far away.

SIX
CALLING DR. RANDOLPH

Unendurable weeks followed. Weeks of gloom, weeks of medication for the gout—stuffy, ear-ringing, headache-blasting medication that left Billy spent, debilitated. Weeks of futile hand exercises that tore at the ligaments and ravaged the small muscles, digital gymnastics that seemed to bring no relief. Golf was a far-distant vision, an aching memory.

Billy often takes under his wing some deserving young man who needs a lift. The home at Bonita always has one or more such protégés. At this time a youth by the name of Emory Allen lived with them while he worked toward his bachelor's degree. Emory was a good golfer, and late one afternoon brought home from the links a message from a retired osteopath, a certain Dr. Carl Stillman.

"Bill," Emory said, "Dr. Stillman said to tell you that he knows what's the matter and what to do about it."

For twelve weeks Billy had let medicine happen to him, with no discernible results. His patience was exhausted, his spirits sagging. Emotionally, he was coming in on the back nine, with every hole a double bogey. So what could he lose? Certainly what he was doing now was no good.

"Let's go see him," Billy said.

Emory looked startled. "Now?" he asked. "It's after seven."

Billy stood up. "If he really can help me, I'm already late. Come on, let's go."

They arrived at Dr. Stillman's house about eight. The doctor was all profession, thought nothing of the hour. He found that Billy had partly dislocated a bone in the palm of his hand and had torn a muscle.

"You see, Billy," he explained. "It's just like the keystone of an arch. If the supporting pillars are jammed up, the keystone has to give. That's what happened to your hand."

The bone was out of place, forcing the muscles and tendons out of their usual channels. Dr. Stillman began manipulating the sore member. The whole hand throbbed by now. The pain was pure torture. Dr. Stillman pressed one of the "pillars," and Bill bit hard on a scream. "Now if I can only hold onto this while I catch the other one," Dr. Stillman said, grunting.

Once more he twisted, turned, manipulated. Red-hot streaks of pain shot through the torn ligaments. Suddenly there was a loud crack. Relief flooded Bill, and he nearly went limp.

"That's got it!" the doctor cried triumphantly. "Now take it easy so it doesn't slip."

For a week he treated Billy twice daily. All the muscles had to be massaged to return the circulation, after the bone snapped back into place. For one more week he worked over the sore wrist once a day. And then he told Billy he was ready to try a club. And so Billy, Dr. Stillman, and Emory went out on the course. Billy returned in triumph, jubilant that he could play again, and play well.

Billy had been off the tour for fourteen weeks. He returned

to the Hartford. He started the last day five strokes behind the leader, big George Bayer. He caught up with Bayer on the fifteenth, where Bayer bogeyed and Billy birdied. Again on the seventeenth, Billy birdied to take a one-shot lead. On the eighteenth, his bid for a birdie from 8 feet missed by 2 inches. But he got his par four and won by one stroke, a comeback champion. He scored 67, 68, 71, 65—271. And the newspaper picture showing the tears of happiness in Shirley's eyes as she leaned against the seated Billy, her face resting on his head, is a heart-clutching sight.

Here again is proof of Billy's prescience, his intuition. He knew he was going to win the Hartford even though the odds were against it, especially after his three-month layoff. He announced he was going to win, which his fellow-pros later attested to. Billy has the power of not looking back but taking things as they unfold. He said, "I've won some good tournaments, but I expect to win more. I feel my peak won't really be reached for three or four years."

About the Hartford, he said, "I putted fantastically." This was not bragging, but a statement of fact. He had a certain firm detachment from himself, and he looked upon his playing from the vantage of this detachment. Also, concerning his putting, a Hartford sportswriter, Don Clerkin said, "Though Billy's putter is the most effective weapon in his golf arsenal, the other thirteen clubs are not impotent blunderbusses."

In spite of his layoff, his hand injury, and ear infection, even with the constant worry over the health of little Billy, and with only twenty starts, he played so consistently well that he won his second Vardon Trophy. He also played on his second Ryder Cup team. Of the 231 tournaments he'd played in as a pro, he'd won 21. Financially, he was eleventh highest money-winner that year, with $32,726.19.

Billy's playing philosophy was in the making. These principles are still with him today. He said in 1963, "A golfer needs to pace himself." Again: "He needs plenty of rest on tour. But most important, a golfer must be willing to get away from it all." This is not easy. Tournament sponsors expect winners to play. Winners are the big drawing cards, and sponsors object strenuously if they do not show. But Billy feels he must get his mind off golf every six or seven weeks to develop a proper balance between trying too hard and relaxing. How does he know when to quit? Del Taylor, his caddy and longtime friend, who probably knows Billy better than almost anyone, says, "When Billy loses his desire to play, it's time for him to rest." Which brings to mind that cogent earlier sentence of Billy's: "It's a desire you have. That's all it is."

Though the wrist injury had healed, the unidentifiable anxiety and moodiness still remained. Billy was depressed when he had no cause to be, and occasionally gay, also without reason. The malaise, the backaches, the headaches, churned within him, continuing the mercurial scoring noted before. His early-morning games were especially bothersome.

At the Los Angeles Open in January 1964, he failed to qualify, shooting a 74, 76. At the San Diego the next week he tied for forty-fourth! At the Bing Crosby he swung the other way, but not far enough, tying for tenth. At the Lucky International and also at the Palm Springs, he tied for seventh. He failed to qualify for the Phoenix. At New Orleans he was down to a tie for twenty-third, and at Pensacola he tied for forty-third. With this erratic record, in March he came to the Doral Open at Miami.

The fourth round was a tough head-to-head battle with Jack Nicklaus. Top bucket was $7,500. On the 437-yard eighteenth, Casper was two ahead. Jack's second shot was 20 feet from the hole. Billy was in the sandtrap. A bogey stared at him. Jack came over and started talking. A spectator remarked, "He's trying to upset Casper." And it did look it when Billy hit a poor trap shot. Jack missed his putt by inches, and Billy took his bogey, winning at 70, 70, 67, 70—277.

Later, when asked what Jack said to him after his second

shot, Billy laughed. "Oh, we talked about fishing all the way around."

The conversation of champions!

Fishing is one of the loves of Bill's life. When he arrives at the site of a new tournament and calls to find out how the course is, he often asks, "How's the fishing?" Whenever he returns to Bonita, he immediately goes deep-sea fishing. (Incidentally, as a perfect *non sequitur*, when he was a boy he caught his first fish using a piece of bread as bait.)

Fishing is his pleasure, but golf is his business. He does not, however, make of it a life-and-death thing. He doesn't do that with anything. His philosophy is that once you've hit a ball, there's nothing you can do about it. "Moaning won't help a poor shot, or body English drop an off-the-line putt." And about people who think putting is his only forte: "You can't putt from the tee. You can't hit the second shot till you've hit the first."

Golf is a game of frustrating extremes, of winning a tournament one week, and missing the cut the next. But there is also the fascination of it. Billy says, "You've got to believe in yourself to win. But it's equally important to understand your limitations." Billy thinks every play. He plays it safe. He doesn't go for broke, doesn't try to get as close to the cup as possible. He concentrates heavily, goes within himself.

The slow buildup of allergens continued. His irritability increased, and he had several bad incidents with spectators. There had been evidence of this before. At Gleneagles, in Chicago, two weeks after his U.S. Open win, Billy had to park some distance from the course and he became furious. So furious, in fact, that he said, "I feel like packing up my clubs and leaving."

Frank Stranahan—who had led the field the first day back at LaBatt in 1956, the year Billy won it—replied to Billy's threat to leave, "I'll give you $100 if you will."

The Greater Greensboro Open found Billy tied for thirtieth. This cellar position was partly erased when the next week Billy tied for fifth at the Masters. At the Tournament of Champions, where pain had become a vulture the preceding year, he tied for twelfth. At the Colonial, in May, disturbances hampered all the pros. First, a lallygagging helicopter hovered over the fairway on the last day. In the leading threesome were Casper, Littler, and Wall. At the sixth hole, the helicopter landed nearby, rattling crowd and players alike. And on the back nine it came after them again. While Billy was making his second shot on the fourteenth, the helicopter banked above him and the blast caused Billy to shank his ball, which stopped just short of the trap. Then Casper canned a fine 12-foot putt for his par. Later he called it the key putt for the round.

The helicopter landed on the first fairway (fortunately after the last threesome had passed) and sat there sphinxlike the rest of the day. Rumors circulated among the gallery: maybe it was Bing Crosby, maybe Bob Hope. But it turned out to be two showgirls who rented the craft because it was hard to see on the ground.

"Fun-lovers," the club manager said airily. "Yesterday they came in an ambulance."

Another disturbance was portable radios. Billy said, laughing: "There must have been 857 radios out there today and all of them were turned on. Every time I was trying to concentrate on my own shot, I was being told what everyone else on the course was doing."

Ordinarily a contestant does not know what the other players are doing, except for those in his own foursome. When a golfer is under par his score on the big board is recorded in red. When he is over par, it is entered in black. This seems backward to most people, who spend their lives scrabbling to "stay out of the red." Billy said of the last day, "As long as I saw that red, I felt good. The only time I lost red was on ten when I three-putted."

On the opening day, Gary Player led with a 68, while Billy had a 72. Arnold Palmer, Masters' winner for the year, shot a

71. Jack Nicklaus, who had won the Tournament of Champions just the week before, slid back to match Billy at 72. Ben Hogan, at that time winner of more Colonial money than anyone, shot a 72, which he was to repeat on the next two days.

In the final round, Billy took the lead with a birdie on the first hole. He never lost it. He and Jacobs entered the last round with 209's. But Jacobs blew to three bogeys on the first six holes and never recovered, finishing second at four behind. The only others who were close were Gary Player and Gene Littler. Littler started the day at 210, one behind Casper. But trouble with back-to-back holes on the front nine dropped him out of contention. Player never got within four strokes and stumbled to a 74. Billy won $14,000, which was $2,000 more than his U.S. Open win and his biggest check to date. He shot 72, 67, 70, 70—279.

Incidentally, the Colonial concluded on Mother's Day. As Billy rolled forward to the winner's circle to receive his big check, the TV camera picked him up. When he took the slip of paper he waved it in the air and called out, "Happy Mother's Day, Shirley."

Two weeks later, in Tennessee, the Memphis Open had some unusual incidents. And though Billy didn't win the Memphis (he tied for second with a 69, 63, 69, 70—271), he did hit one of his best shots, one worth talking about. But first, a few of those unusual happenings. In that tournament the air was filled with flying feathers. Bob Duden had a double eagle, and there were enough plain eagles and birdies to fill an aerie. There were sub-par scores by the score. Tony Lema played with a bum back that at one point threatened to put him out of the tournament. But he played extremely well, and at the halfway mark stood fourth. And the current British Open champion, Bob Charles, screamed a shattering first-nine of 28! Bob addresses his ball from the south, and all left-handed golfers stood 10 feet tall that night. But the biggest thrill of the tournament occurred on the second day on the eighteenth hole. It is a par-five hole that Billy eagled. He rimmed the cup with a 90-foot wedge shot that clung precariously, then dropped. An ill wind which blew good. Billy carded a 63 for the day.

But this good shot, even this win, was still cyclic in his overall pattern. Billy's putter grew temperamental on him. Earlier he had dubbed his putter "Sweet Charity" because it covered "such a multitude of sins from tee to green." But Sweet Charity had soured. And as his caddy, Del, said, "When his putter goes bad on him, Billy's in trouble."

At the 1964 Open, in Washington, D.C., Billy said, "I just don't putt a lick anymore. I score as well as ever because I play better. But I don't putt as well. If I could get a putting streak going, I might win this tournament. Because there's no comparison between my game now and in 1959, when I won the Open." He finished fourth. Gary Player said, "I feel sorry for Casper. He can't putt a lick. He missed three 30-footers out there today."

Bill's headaches became staggering. Everything on the course bothered him. He used up a big bottle of aspirin every few weeks. He was sickly. Shirley, too, was overweight, and she suffered from edema and migraine. Young Billy was also overweight, and required constant gamma-globulin shots.

Bill had another source of distress—Shirley's younger brother, John. In the fall of 1963, Granny and her second family, young John and younger Margee, had moved in with the Caspers. Granny needed a new home at the time, and living on Spanish Hill in Bonita, Granny could better watch over the growing Casper brood. John was a quiet boy, handsome, a year older than little Billy, and a good playmate for Billy. But in the spring of 1964, John became withdrawn, separate, needing no one. It was typical of Billy that his wife's brother became at once a child in his home and Bill's responsibility. And Bill worried over Johnny's introversion. No longer did Johnny like to rough-and-tumble with young Billy. He preferred his toy soldiers, which were almost a passion with him. Granny became depressed, and the malaise seemed to spread all through her. To Bill, it seemed as if illness dogged his entire family, and it harrowed his peace of mind.

In 1960 he had met Bill and Laura Kerr, from New York City. Staunch friends, they had tried many times to persuade Billy to go to a Dr. Theron G. Randolph of Chicago. The Kerrs had come to the Caspers in 1961 with glowing accounts of the benefits they had received from this internationally known allergist. At this time Granny was suffering from deep depression, and Bill and Shirley were greatly worried. They determined to go to Chicago for testing. But somehow it never happened, and they continued on tour. In 1962 Billy promised the Kerrs he really would go this time, and he was ready to go in the fall. But the Cuban crisis fired the world, and Granny and the children back in Bonita were worried, and asked the Caspers to return home from the perilous (to them) bomb-threatened environs of New York. Again in 1963 the Caspers promised the Kerrs they would be tested for sensitivity. But Billy hurt his wrist and was plagued by his severe ear infection. His doctors in San Diego warned him not to fly, because of the ear infection, and urged him not to go.

At the Western, in Chicago, in August 1964, the Caspers finally made good their promise to their friends. During the tournament, Shirley and the children went through Dr. Randolph's tests. And one week later, Billy was tested. For several years, Billy had complained that every morning when he approached the first tee, he became sleepy. At night he would roll and toss, restless and upset. Sleep came harder than a 30-foot putt. And the next morning Billy would come out for a tournament depressed and irritable. Mostly, the excitement of competitive play would throw off his lethargy. But often during the tournament he would be nearly overcome by his need for rest. And as soon as possible he would lie down. Though his eyes would close, and his mind would quiet, the accompanying sleep would be as if he were drugged. He would find no relief from it, except that he would experience just enough of the tense sleep to rob him of his rest at night. This vicious circle, which usually occurs only in a much older person, gradually wore Billy down. His moodiness became belligerent, and it all seemed to be centered on that early-morning approach to the first tee.

And no wonder! After Dr. Randolph completed his subcutaneous test injections, the allergist discovered that Billy had seven pronounced allergens—items that are customarily eaten at breakfast. These were: wheat (toast), citrus, eggs, peas and beans, pork (bacon, ham), chocolate, and peanuts. Though Billy rarely ate peanuts for breakfast, the other items were all standard and made up what Dr. Randolph jokingly referred to as the "All-American breakfast." Thus every day before going out to play, Billy would partake of two, three, or even more foodstuffs that were harmful to him. And the result—he would go to sleep, or spend the first nine holes fighting the desire.

This was far more serious than just a drugged sleep. His nerves became frayed, his game suffered, and his belligerence toward his gallery became almost insufferable. He withdrew within himself, and even Granny, who loved him dearly, dreaded his moods. Often she became impatient with him because she herself was beginning to slip into the despair of an allergic illness. It was on this ominous horizon that Dr. Randolph appeared.

SEVEN
STRIDING ALONG

The hope that springs eternal mounted high within Billy when Dr. Randolph outlined the future: Make the necessary changes in home and traveling environment; avoid certain foods; work out the remaining members of the food families represented. Then his health would return.*

But there is no arsic flow without a thetic. No birdie on the eighteenth without some bogey on the front nine. Blighting Billy's joy over eventual recovery came a long-distance call from Dr. Franklin. Granny was very ill, he suspected cancer, and the Caspers had better return at once. The tour was forgotten as anxious Shirley and Bill flew back.

The hospital disproved the cancer, but Granny was indeed very ill. Her hemoglobin had dropped dangerously, and the hospital gave her a transfusion. She withdrew from society, just as Johnny had withdrawn—except Granny was worse off.

* A detailed discussion of Dr. Randolph's program will be found in the Appendix.

She locked her door, refused to see anyone. Depressed, in semihysteria, she had lost her will to live. And Bill sensed this. After a dramatic scene of silent communication and eventual calm reassurances, Bill persuaded Granny to go to Dr. Randolph.

With Granny well taken care of, and with little Billy working out his own allergies, Bill returned to the tour. He tied for eighth at the Carling, and for third at Dallas. At "Caspertown," the Portland Open, he came in sixth.

Rarely has one man carried such a burden, especially through a task requiring so much calm and concentration. His own health was still in a precarious state, a sensitized state. Shirley, too, was in the working-out phase, where the least departure from regimen would cause great discomfort and difficulty. Young Billy was at home, under good care, but still a deep worry because the impact of the program on his hypo-gamma-globulin anemia was still a moot point—to Shirley and Bill, that is. Dr. Randolph had assured them the boy would recover completely. And Granny lay in the hospital in Chicago, in deep despair.

With this load of anxiety, Billy approached the Seattle Open in September of 1964. The worries registered, and on the final day, Billy was three strokes off the pace. Behind him two strokes was Mason Rudolph, from Tennessee. Al Geiberger and Fred Marti were the third-round leaders, tied at 199. It was a beautiful day, and the Broadmoor course was at its best, sunlit and dotted with maple trees. Billy plodded steadily along, playing his consistent, thinking golf. No thought of the gallery, no thought of anything but the ball and the pin. An occasional jagged reminder of Granny. On the sixteenth he caught a maple tree, but five-ironed his way out of trouble and got down in par. Geiberger slipped to a 69, and Marti skidded to a 73. Billy carded a final 64, finishing 265, fifteen under par. Rudolph also turned in a 64, which though it included a hole-in-one gave him only second place at 267.

Billy had six birdies, and his 265 was the lowest 72-hole score of the year in tournament golf.

People often wonder what golfers think of each other. Rarely is there a chance to find out. After the Seattle Open in 1964, Byron Nelson wrote a most illuminating column on Billy.

There may be some people who beat Bill Casper on the golf course. But Bill will never beat himself. Some people, including some of our golfers, are their own worst enemies. Bill is his own best friend. He is . . . unique. . . . He plays more like a man going to the office than anybody I know. It's just a day's work for Bill, and he doesn't let it get the best of him.

Bill works less on his game than anyone on the tour. He feels it takes the edge off if he practices like the others. He says, "I can get just as much out of a half-hour on the practice tee as I get out of a whole practice round."

Bill does what he feels like doing. He always impresses me as a man who knows he's going to be playing the next year, the next year, and the next year, and the next. And you can expect him to be one of our finest players as long as he keeps this splendid attitude.

Bill plays in only about twenty-five tournaments a year. "When I stay around the tour too long, everything starts bothering me," Casper said. "When that happens, it's time to go home."

This corroborates the opinion of his caddy, Del Taylor.

In October, just six weeks after Billy first saw Dr. Randolph, Jack Murphy of the *San Diego Union*, made the first reference to Billy's loss of weight. He spoke of "the svelte Billy Casper, with his 18-pound loss." This tone was in decided contrast to previous newspaper comments and gallery ribbings. At the Kentucky Derby, in 1959, a spectator had said, "Billy sure is crabby. I hear he takes cortisone every morning for his bad elbow." At the Crosby in 1960, on the fourth hole, Billy whacked a terrific drive. From the following crowd came a caustic comment: "Old Jelly-Belly really laid into that one, didn't he?" Again, later: "Billy must really be

a boozer! Look at that fat stomach." Another time, two elderly
men were arguing whether Billy was Casper or not. "Naw,
that couldn't be Casper." "Yes it is. I read he was on a diet."
"Yeah, but not that much." They made a wager, and then
asked Billy. He pulled out his driver's license and showed
them. But perhaps the most unusual doubt of his identity came
from Shirley. In company with a family friend, she was following Billy around Harding Park, in San Francisco. Billy
was in the middle of the fairway. Shirley turned to her friend.
"Where's Bill? Did his group go through?" The friend pointed
out onto the course. "No," he said. "That's Bill over there."

The Almaden Open, at San Jose, was one of those typical
high-intensity last-minute charges that leave spectators breath-
less and writers flapping for adjectives. The weather was a
plaguing distress, blustery, with rain and obnoxious winds.
The tournament lagged a day late. The start of the third
round had to be postponed until 10 A.M., with the field split,
half on the back nine, half on the front. On the 54th hole, a
rookie, Chuck Courtney, held the lead with a 70, and a total
of 208. He was just one slap ahead of Charlie Sifford and
Jerry Steelsmith, who had led the first two rounds. Three were
tied back at 210: U.S. Open winner Ken Venturi, with a
sparkling 67; Pete Brown, the first Negro ever to win an
official PGA-sponsored tournament, who also had a 67; and
smooth-swinging Sam Carmichael. Billy was next, all by himself at 211, three strokes off the pace. His first two days had
been a 68 and 70, but the third day he slipped to a 73.

But as Joe Wilmot put it, "Putting master Casper is the
kind of a guy who dotes on hiding in the weeds and knocking
off the sheriff just as he reaches the pass." So, on the fourth
day, Monday, there was a three-way tie. Billy, Pete Brown,
and Steelsmith all hung up a 279 for the regulation 72 holes.

Tuesday was election day, November 4. But always politic-
conscious, Billy had foreseen the possibility of this, and had
cast his absentee ballot. The threesome started out on the
eighteen-hole playoff. At the end of the first nine, Pete Brown

was leader with a sizzling three-under-par 33. He had three birds, on the fifth, sixth, and ninth. Casper had birds on the fifth and ninth, to go out on a 34. Steelsmith clipped his only birdie of the playoff on the ninth, a 6-footer for 35. The tension was tremendous. They had played four full days, and even at the end of the first nine on the fifth day, they were still all bunched in a Gordian knot.

Steelsmith cut the knot with bogeys on the tenth and eleventh. Brown and Casper kept up the head-on battle, Pete still one ahead. On the thirteenth hole, 545 yards, Billy drew even with Brown with a 5-foot birdie putt, and both were three under. On the fourteenth, Brown sank a 25-footer for a birdie three to the delight of the gallery. The "Ahs" were a soft blessing on the afternoon air. Billy caught Pete again on the sixteenth by canning a 12-footer for a bird, and each man parred the seventeenth. And so they reached the dramatic eighteenth, still even, after 89 holes!

Casper was on in a regulation two, but Brown clobbered his shot to the base of a tree to the right of the green. Pete and his caddy studied the shot for a long time. Then Pete swung mightily, trying to fade his shot around the tree. He got too much muscle into it and the ball sailed clear over the green, bounced between a couple of spectators, and came to rest on the macadam behind the hole. But Pete made a fine chip shot, and then, with the pressure mounting, he sank a 2-footer and saved his par to send the match into the sudden-death playoff. They tied at four under for 68.

Wearily, the two men plodded over to the first sudden-death hole—was ever a torture so exquisitely named! They had already completed ninety greens. They were dead-tired, under severe strain. Yet Billy found time to praise Brown. "Pete ranks with any of the long hitters in the game today. Don't let anyone tell you Pete can't putt. You saw those snakes he made when the chips were down. He is one of the best I've seen—and he'll get nothing but better."

On the first hole of the sudden-death, both players missed

long putts that would have settled the issue pronto. They halved the hole with par-fives. On the second hole, Brown, who had been a putting sensation all day, stretched out the long duel with a fine recovery wedge from off the right of the green. He tapped in a dead-eye 8-footer for another par-saver. The third hole—actually, the ninety-third!—was 415 yards of real tension. Billy's second shot was a seven-iron that started to the right, then turned and skidded to within 6 feet of the pin. Brown was also on the carpet in two, but his approach was 25 feet short of the flag. On his try for an equalizing birdie, he was 18 inches short. Billy clipped his 6-footer with ease. It must have been the buffalo steaks and home-canned rhubarb he'd eaten for breakfast.

The day had seen tremendous golf for both. And neither Casper nor Brown made a bogey in the entire playoff. Billy said, "It's the finest 21 holes of golf I've ever played. Imagine! I hit all 21 greens; I've never done that before. And no bogeys all day. This Almaden course is the best I've played on all year."

It was the twenty-fifth tournament win of Billy's career. In his ten years as a pro, he'd played in a total of 263 tournaments, 32 that year. He'd been in the money 26 times in the 32, and had won four. He was the third highest money-winner for the year, with $90,653.08. His total winnings since turning pro were $372,072.27.

On December 16, 1964, San Diego saluted its most famous golfing son by celebrating Billy Casper Day. Mayor Frank Curran read the official proclamation. Over three hundred friends and well-wishers attended. Messages came from all over the country, from Congressmen, military leaders, Hollywood personalities. The program consisted of people who had known and befriended Billy in his early days. His original backers were there, dressed in poverty-shrieking rags. One announced, "I used to drive a Lincoln Continental." "What do you drive now?" the other sponsor asked. "A couple of burros," the first replied. The house cracked up. Young Billy mimed his father as the boy out on the cow pasture. Bob Reynolds said, in a short burst of praise, "Billy is one of the top five golfers, and will be one of the great ones of our era." Then he told the story of the two-iron shot at the 1962 Bing Crosby. "Walking away from the second green, Billy tapped his putter against a fence. Not hard or in anger. But it was cold, and the head broke off. Shirley asked how far to the clubhouse. She was going to get another putter. I replied, 'I'm no authority on rules. But I'm pretty sure he has to play out the round with the clubs he started with.' Billy made his drive from the third tee. Then he drew out a two-iron and said, 'This is my putter.' On the remaining sixteen greens, he used it as if he'd never putted with anything else. He finished one under par. The following day at Pebble Beach, with a new putter, he set a course record of 65."

The next year began with Billy afire. On the first day of the Los Angeles Open, he was in one of his supreme putting streaks. He decorated his scorecard with five birdies and not a single bogey. Most of the time he was on in regulation figures and down in two putts. Some of the putts were whoppers.

At the par-three third he sank a 30-footer for a deuce. On the eleventh he rammed home a 70-footer and the crowd blasted the fairway with its approval. On the twelfth he saved his par-three with a 12-foot slapdown. He cupped a 20-footer at sixteen, and on the final hole slammed his second shot stiff to the pin for a 3½-foot birdie. He led the pack at 66.

On the second day he slipped to a 72, tying with Dan Sikes at 138 for the 36 holes. But though he had lost 30 pounds since his last appearance at the Los Angeles, and though he breakfasted on fresh salmon and home-canned plums, Billy couldn't evade the three bogeys that lay in wait on the back nine. He said, "I didn't play badly, but I couldn't get the feel of my putter." And as has been pointed out, when Billy loses his friendship with Sweet Charity, he's in trouble.

Casper was among the early starters, teeing off in the

hardly-awake hours. Somebody asked him if the frost on the ground bothered him. "No," he grinned. "But the frost in my swing sure did."

On the final day, Billy had trouble at the eighth. A drainage ditch nearly swallowed his ball. But Billy has always been one of golf's best trouble-shooters. And true to his reputation, Billy chipped out for a par-five. He finished with a 71, good enough for third place and $4,000. Paul Harney successfully defended, winning at 276.

San Diego, the next week, was as tightly climactical as any gasper. Billy had never won his hometown tournament, and he had his heart and his magic putter set on it. The gallery turned out larger than ever before at the Stardust Country Club. Emotions were mixed for the San Diego crowd: they had nine local boys to root for. In his gold cap and sweater and charcoal brown slacks, Billy topped the list of favorites. But the remainder of the San Diego stable contained some strong names: Littler, Phil Rodgers, Al Geiberger, Larry Mowry, and the newest local hot-shot, Chuck Courtney. To add local color as well as prestige, the others were former National PGA champion Paul Runyun, Don Whitt, and Bill Nary. Both Rodgers and Littler were battling the tail end of a drought duststorm—eighteen months without a victory for Rodgers, and nearly three years for Littler. Chuck Courtney had almost copped the rookie-of-the-year award, having been nosed out by Dick Sikes. The gallery hoped they'd be paired. Defending champion was Art Wall.

Billy was riding high. On the first three days he shot a 70, 68, and a 65. The fourth day he breakfasted on fresh papaya and green peppers stuffed with ground bear. He went out ready to roar. But on the eighth hole he missed a 2-foot birdie putt. It was to cost him the tournament, though the match was to go on to a sudden-death. "There was a little strip of high grass running from me to the hole," he recalled afterward. "It looked like something the mower missed. I hit a little hard, trying to get the ball over the high grass, trying to stuff it in the hole. Only time all day I tried to stuff one in. If I'd have shot easier, I'd have made it." The ball curled around the rim of the cup, then came out. And after twelve holes, Billy was six under par for the round and two strokes ahead of Ellis. "I guess I started coasting a little then," Billy said. "I played thirteen, fourteen, and fifteen safely. I didn't continue to attack as I had been doing. I probably should have." Billy had seven birdies and no bogies. These included putts of 45 and 35 feet. The only birdie putt he missed was the 2-footer on the eighth that cost him the tournament. He finished with a 70, 68, 65, 64—267, seventeen under par, which score broke by two the tournament record established by Mike Souchak in 1960. It looked as if Billy had the tournament zippered shut.

As Billy finished eighteen, Wes Ellis and Johnny Pott were on the seventeenth tee, 398 yards away. Billy made his final birdie, putting both Ellis and Pott two strokes behind with two to play. Ellis had led the field the first two days. And Pott three times had been runner-up in this tournament. On the seventeenth, both birdied, Ellis with a 15-foot putt. Now if either or both could birdie the final hole, it would force the match into a sudden-death playoff.

Pott slammed the ball within 15 feet of the cup. Ellis's lie was 48 feet short, off in the grass at the front edge of the green. He studied it for a long time. So much depended on it. At last he addressed the ball and smacked it.

The ball began its cross-country roll. Hypnotized, Billy stared at the traveling sphere. If it stayed out of the cup—and that appeared probable, since the distance was 48 feet—he, Casper, would be winner of the thirteenth San Diego Open, his cherished dream. If it went in, there would be a tie and a sudden-death.

The ball rolled and rolled and rolled across the smooth green turf. Suddenly, when the ball was still 20 feet from the hole, Casper gasped and said, "He made it!" while the ball was still rolling.

The pill seemed to gather speed, and it struck the can dead-center, jumped in the air for a heartbreaking moment, then plopped in. The gallery went mad. Ellis had a 267. Later he said, "When I hit it I was sure of only one thing—that it would be long enough. If it hadn't hit the hole dead center, it would have gone 4 or 5 feet past."

The tension blistered upward as the contenders, followed by their galleries, plodded across the fairway to the first green for the seventy-third hole. Sudden-death! The playoff hole was 347 yards. Ellis drove first, well down the fairway. Casper's drive was 10 feet farther. Ellis played a nine-iron 6 feet to the right of the cup. Billy used a sand-iron from a grassy fairway lie. The ball took off flying and didn't stop until it was beyond the back of the green, 18 feet from the hole. Casper putted bare inches past the cup. Ellis went into his wide putting stance and sank the putt. Bedlam!

An unforgettable gallery comment occurred right then, the kind that remains great and you wished you had spotted the speaker. A spectator muttered, "The lamb just slew the butcher."

One of the most revealing scenes of Billy-the-family-man occurred here. Throughout the tournament young Billy had been following his father on the fairway, the boyish eyes glowing with hero-worship. Rarely does a boy so identify with his father as does son Billy. When Wes Ellis triumphed in the sudden-death, young Billy witnessed the deciding shot. The gallery cheered, but the boy lowered his head against his father and broke into tears. Bill held him at arm's length. "It's easy to be a good winner, son," he said. "You have to learn to be a good loser, too."

Then Bill congratulated Ellis on his playing, put his arm around his son, and walked off.

The Bob Hope Golf Classic came early in February. With Billy's new figure, which all the sportswriters were commenting on. Bob called him the "Solid Ry-Krisp." High purse was $15,000. The first day's topper was Frank Beard and the second-day flag-wavers were Kermit Zarley and club-pro

Stan Thirsk. The third-day pace-setter was Rod Funseth, who had played the PGA tour regularly for three years without causing any fast pulses. But the third day, he shot a one-under-par 71 at La Quinta for a leading 206, ten under par.

The Bob Hope was not then an official PGA tournament, though it is today. The match was and still is one of the greatest challenges that the professionals encounter. There are five rounds, played on four difficult courses: La Quinta, Indian Wells, Bermuda Dunes, and—often considered the toughest—Eldorado. Each golfer plays each of these courses once. And in 1965, the final (fifth) round was a repeat of Bermuda Dunes.

The year before, Billy came to the fifth round tied, but he slipped on the last eighteen holes as Tommy Jacobs came through to nudge Jimmy Demaret in the playoff. But in 1965, Jacobs was lost in the shuffle at 226, and Demaret had been disqualified earlier for missing a starting time.

Billy's fourth round was a spanking 67, five under par. He was two shots ahead of Frank Beard, the first day's leader, and three shots ahead of Arnold Palmer. He fought winds and a few sprinkles of rain, carding six birdies and two bogies. Twice he flopped in a trap, one resulting in a bogey, the other in a par. The second and third days' unknowns slid back to their accustomed hermitages, and the big boys tramped forth.

The final drama occurred as always on the eighteenth hole. Palmer was already in with a 70, though Billy didn't know that, and it wouldn't have bothered him had he known it. He plays his game, not the other man's. Billy had a wonderful drive, at least 280 yards. His second shot was the key shot, a four-wood for 240 yards. This left him about 40 feet from the cup. He putted to within 3 feet, then sank the pill for a birdie and his first win of the year. The late President Eisenhower described the putt as a "knee-knocker."

Billy had Sunday problems after the win: He could not cash the $15,000 check; and he was without a driver for the new car that went with the win, since he'd brought his own automobile to the tournament. A friend volunteered to take the wheel of the new car. On the way back to Bonita, the Highway Patrol pinched the entire cavalcade for doing an exultant 80.

After the Bob Hope Classic, the next week at Phoenix, Billy was paired with Barry Goldwater for the Pro-Am. On the sixth, Goldwater pulled his ball to the left and hit a spectator. This is one of the hazards that haunt all golfers, and Billy is no exception. The spectator had to be stitched up at the hospital. (Whether this came as ironic justice for Goldwater, because he switched to the left, is not known.) Billy tied for 12th to win $1,550.

He had not intended to play Tucson this year, but because of the success of his program, as symbolized by the breakfasts that the newspapers always commented on—because of his general good health he did go on to Tucson, where he came in fourth.

By this time the newspapers were full of comments on Billy's weight loss. It was the most obvious result of the Randolph program, but not the most important. The biggest thing Dr. Randolph gave to Billy was returning health, and with it a highly improved, more consistent, less erratic golf game. In March, as he readied for the Doral, Billy said, "Who loves a fat man? Nobody. He may bowl them over at office parties, but on the golf course he's just a big slop—a nothing." He had slimmed down from a puffing 230 to a trim 190.

It was most fortunate that he had lost weight, even though he didn't try to do so. Otherwise he would have followed Grandpa Casper's painful path. When Grandpa was twenty-two he weighed 210 pounds. By 1920, when he was thirty-six, Grandpa bulled over the scale at 350 pounds. As he became older he churned the surroundings with irascibility. Coupled with his domineering nature, this irritability made his disposition unbearable. During his last three years he became blind. He was under sedation the last three months, and he died in

June 1946. He still weighed 290 pounds, despite the wasting away of terminal illness. The cause of death was uremic poisoning, and the autopsy showed possibilities also of hepatitis. But Billy has dodged all this misery because he has identified his allergens and is successfully avoiding them. He discovered the cause of his obesity, and did something about it.

Approaching Doral's Blue Monster Course, Billy was the prime favorite. All accounts spoke of his slim figure, his awareness, his keenness, his eagerness to play. He'd defeated the Blue Monster twice before—in 1962 and 1964. Even the Fearsome Four, that 225-yard hole where only forty-five par-threes had been made the last two rounds in 1964—even the Fearsome Four held no menace, though the rest of the pros objected strongly to the hole.

But something went wrong. Perhaps it was a return of the cyclic scoring, the ups-and-downs that marked his before-Randolph playing. Or, much more likely, it was the insidious turning up of additional allergens. The secondary allergens, they are called. After the first allergens are identified, and by means of the working-out phase of the program are avoided, secondary allergens make their appearance. Not as cogent as the primary ones, they make their presence known because the effects of the primary allergens are no longer present to mask the secondaries. It's a vicious circle. At any rate, Billy suddenly went into a slump. He tied for twenty-ninth. The Blue Monster had clawed him down.

Depressed, he went on to Jacksonville the next week. During the first three holes, Billy had heart palpitations and nearly passed out. Perhaps years of overweight had weakened his heart, leaving it a vulnerable link in his system. Allergens seek out such points with almost fiendish accuracy. Suddenly Billy blacked out. He came to, then nearly conked out again. They hurried a golf cart across the fairway and brought him in. The doctor diagnosed it as P.A.T.—paratachycardia, and administered a pill containing, among other things, potassium. Shirley rushed Billy to Dr. Randolph, back in Chicago. More tests showed a somewhat confused reaction to lamb and apples. Chemicals were not suspect at this time.

Though Billy tied for second at Greensboro the first week in April, his spirits were on the ebb again, and all his friends were worried. The papers made much of his breakfasts (strange, since the other meals were equally important), and reported he had shrimp and plums the first day, and a Cornish hen and avocado with tea the second, and so on. Though his take of $4,733.33 easily paid for these exotic breakfasts, the depression that struck him was virulent.

Before the Masters he said, "I've gotten more publicity this year than ever before. Not for my golf, but for my diet. I'm grateful for the program, but I'm a sound golfer, too. I actually feel my putting is the worst part of it. In order to finish among the top-ten money-winners you have to have a sound game. You can't rely on any one facet of it." He felt he was ready for the Masters. He loved the course, and the Masters was a cherished dream he'd never won. That bright green coat which traditionally goes to the winner! Yes, this year, his best so far, he was all set. Yet, temperamentally, he felt lower than a double bogey, he was suspicious of his friends, rude and arrogant to those he'd just met. And he flopped in the Masters, tying for thirty-fourth. He was not the Billy his loved ones knew.

His anger deepened. He began to be boorish to his old friends, the Kerrs. Actually, he was punishing himself, and in a vicious circle was accusing himself of the actual errors and bad plays he was committing. By tacit consent, everyone turned to Granny, source of strength for the family. Some of his friends begged her to intervene. Shirley implored, "Speak to him, Mama."

"The kids are my job, Bill's yours," Granny replied.

"I'm too close to him. I counsel him all the time. You could be more objective. Couldn't you talk to him, just this once?"

Laura Kerr pleaded, "That boy hurts! Can't you do something?" His game deteriorated: tied for thirty-second at

Houston, tied for sixth at the Tournament of Champions (a little sunlight on a dark time), tied for twenty-second at the Colonial, and on and on.

On a flying visit home, he snarled his way around the house, and after a bit of soul-searching Granny did talk to him. At this moment, to her he was just like any of the five little children she counseled and disciplined daily.

"Bill," she said, "each man is a principality. And he must bring his principality into order, otherwise there is anarchy, and the person is at odds with himself. Bill, I'm going to pray for you."

Bill, whose interest in the Mormon Church had by now become profound, acquiesced without words.

Granny believes firmly in prayer and the power of prayer. She asked her minister how she could help Bill. The minister told her to pray for Bill's self-acceptance. Further, Granny was to repeat this prayer every time Bill came into her thoughts, which was often indeed. Granny did this many times a day from June to December.

Results were not immediate. At Indianapolis, Billy tied for twenty-sixth. At the Buick, he tied for fourteenth. The Cleveland Open dropped him to a tie for twenty-ninth, and the self-flagellation reached new fury. He hated himself, and those around him paid for it. Frightened, Shirley phoned, "Mama, please pray for Bill."

And Granny said, "Stand steady, Shirley. I'll keep on what I'm doing, and you pray with me. Have faith."

For the Western Open, Granny took the children from Bonita to join Shirley and Bill in Chicago. It was a vacation, a lark-trip. But the trip had another purpose—more testing for Shirley and Bill and the Casper children, a follow-up for Granny, and first testing for Johnny and Margee. Bill was in a hellish mood, flailing at everyone, most of all himself. As soon as his children arrived he began to calm down, always the family man. On Sunday morning, after a breakfast of peaches and pheasant, he and little Billy were going down in

the hotel elevator. Young Billy said, "Go out and win it for
me, Daddy." And Billy said, "Okay, son."

And he did just that. He tore the Tam O'Shanter Club
Course to shreds on the last day of its existence. On each of
the first two holes he clipped a birdie putt of 15 feet. On the
305-yard fifth hole his drive plummeted down 10 feet from
the cup. (Who said Casper couldn't drive?) He dropped the
putt for an eagle. He birdied the next hole with a 10-foot putt
and the following one with a 5-footer. On the first nine he had
a 30, missing the course record by only one stroke, and only
one stroke behind the best nine-hole total on the PGA tour
for the year.

On the back nine he cupped a 15-footer for another birdie
on the eleventh. On the fifteenth he sank his second putt for
another bird. He had his only bogey on the sixteenth, but
made up for it with a final putt of 25 feet on the eighteenth.
His total was 70, 66, 70, 64—270. And after practically every
shot he made, the gallery heard a delighted cry from young
Billy, "That's my daddy!"

When he accepted his winning check, Billy introduced his
family on TV. He referred to Granny as "my wife's mother,"
an affectionate gesture of dignity mentioned earlier. As he did
so, Granny's gaze met Shirley's. Almost in unison they whispered, "Thank you, Father."

Shirley and Granny and Dr. Randolph had started a subtle
plot to hospitalize Bill right after the tournament. The doctor
wanted him to go through the fast, the most definitive testing,
to discover what allergens were causing this latest trouble. But
true to his word to his son that morning in the elevator, Billy
won the Western, and in so doing won the plot. The win made
everybody feel so much better they abandoned the scheme.
Billy did agree to take a third series of tests, which showed a
whole new field of allergens, the dangerous (because insidious) chemical ones. And thus the allergist discovered that the
heart trouble in Jacksonville a few months earlier was not primarily caused by the maligned lamb and apples, but by the

chemical sprays that had been used on the course a few days
before. The potassium that was in the pill the doctor prescribed down in Florida actually did bring relief, but not as a
heart remedy. The benefit came because potassium is a neutralizer and anti-allergen. And this enabled Billy to go on to
Dr. Randolph.

At Chicago he had just won $11,000 and the Western with
a fourteen-under-par 270. He gave due credit to Dr. Randolph
and the program. The doctor had by now found ten allergens:
citrus, wheat, pork, eggs, peas, beans, chocolate, lamb, beet
sugar, and apples. And the insidious omnipresent chemicals.

At the Insurance City Open three weeks later Billy caught
a virus that Shirley had picked up at Toronto the week before
and passed on to young Billy. The virus weakened Bill. He
was awake all Thursday night and hadn't eaten for two days.
Even so, he shot a 70 and 72 the first two rounds. Then the
virus left and he began to return to normal. However, the
temperature rose, and for the last two rounds he faced stifling
heat and humidity. But the golfer that is inherent in the man
took over and he carded two 66's, finishing tied with Johnny
Pott at 274, ten under par. The sudden-death playoff began
immediately on the fifteenth hole. Johnny's second shot barely
made the apron. Billy's was on the green. Pott's shot rimmed
the cup but fell off, and he had to be content with a par four.
This set the stage for Billy's birdie. He was 20 feet from the
pin. If he could sink this one for a birdie, he'd have it made.
He addressed the ball, his slimmed-down frame in his famous
putting stance. He drew back, and the crowd held its breath
in silent respect. Just as his club was about to fall, a six-o'clock
whistle blasted from a nearby fire station. Most golfers would
have screamed their anger. One would have smashed his club.
But a smile came on Billy's face and the tension broke. His
shot flowed easy as running water, true to the hole for a birdie.
It was his forty-third-straight "in-the-money" tournament.

Money was coming in by the barrowful: $11,000 at the
Insurance City Open, followed by $4,500 for his fifth-place

finish at the Thunderbird the next week; at Philadelphia, Billy came in tenth for $2,600; the PGA at Ligonier brought him $12,500 for second place, which was a particular delight, since the winner was his old and close friend Dave Marr.

Dr. Stillman, the osteopath who had salvaged Bill's hand earlier, made a significant and cogent observation at this time. Back in Ligonier, Billy was standing by the broadcaster for the TV release. He was tied with Nicklaus for second. And when it was clear Dave had won, Billy announced over a national hook-up, "I am especially pleased that the tournament should go to my old friend, Dave Marr."

Back in San Diego, Dr. Stillman stated, "There is absolutely no greed in that fellow."

A simple, factual truth.

The Sahara Open in October was another of those constant excitements that make up the life of the touring pro. The first day, Billy carded a 34 going out and a 32 coming in. He had six birdies, three on each nine. Only one bogey. His 66 was five under par for a two-stroke lead. On the second day he repeated the performance, even to the number of birdies and the bogey. This 132 was a tournament record, due no doubt to his breakfast of bear steak with Cranshaw melon. He was three strokes ahead. The third day he breakfasted more in keeping with the rest of America, oatmeal, sliced bananas, and tea. The temperature was a blistering ninety. Billy had four birdies, but still only one bogey, ending with a 68. His total of 200 for the first 54 holes maintained his lead of three.

He began the fourth day with a favorite breakfast, beef liver with natural brown rice, and papaya. On the ninth green the ball hit the back of the cup, spun back, looked in, but remained out. Billy turned away from the ball, feeling it was still moving. Just as he moved up to it again, it proved it was still moving by dropping in for a par four. The delay was about thirty seconds. But the acting PGA tournament director assessed a two-stroke penalty for not knocking the ball in promptly when it hung. Rule 35-1-H requires a player to putt

at once when a ball stops on the edge of the cup. Billy con-
tended his ball was still moving, a statement supported by
Tommy Aaron, a playing partner. The penalty gave Billy a
double-bogey six for the hole. This weirdie ruling will probably remain one of the great unsettled questions in golf, like
Dempsey's long count in boxing. However, the discussion was
purely academic, because even with the two-stroke spanking,
Billy still won by three. His score was a 66, 66, 68, 69–269,
fifteen under par. He lead Martindale by three. He used only
112 putts for the 72 holes, 32 under regulation.

This was his eleventh year of professional golf. He won
the Vardon Trophy for the third time in six years with an
average of 70.586. He was number one on Ryder Cup standings. He finished the year with $99,931.90. For his eleven
years of playing he had made $471,999.17 in 294 tournaments,
of which he had won 29. In 1965 he played in 31 tournaments, winning four, and in the money a total of 27. But far
more important, he finished the year with returning health.
His loved ones—wife Shirley, son Billy, Granny, her young
son John—were also on the highway to happiness. They had
all weathered illnesses, depressions, and severe pain. And now
the open road to life lay ahead.

They invited the Mormon missionaries to come and teach
them the Gospel. It was a time of thanksgiving, a time of
gratitude. A time to restore their faith.

EIGHT
FAMILY HEALTH AND LOVE

Yes, the family was on the upper road. But they'd had an agonized and rugged climb to reach that euphoric ease. First had been young Billy.

Several times in 1959, sudden high fever had struck him inexplicably. His temperature would always drop within a day. Beyond puzzling a bit about it, Shirley put it down to "growing pains," that catch-all illness. Once the doctors found a high lead level, and they thought they traced it to the sticks and leaves he had eaten grublike from the yard. On the basis of our present knowledge, we can guess that these bits of herbaceous chewing gum little Billy indulged in were doubtless recently sprayed by the gardener. And when the three-year-old popped them into his mouth, he actually was ingesting not the lettuce-green leaf and joyous dirty dirt but a poison insidiously creeping into his system.

One morning in April of 1960, Billy went into convulsions soon after awakening. His fever shot up, this time to the astronomical reading of 106! And then he lapsed into unconsciousness. Shirley rushed him to the hospital, where the doctors puzzled over the unknown. They administered antibiotics, not for any special thing but because they didn't really know what to do. They identified it as an infection, but they could not be specific. They gave medication for the fever. All tests were fruitless. The next morning his temperature again dropped mysteriously and Shirley took Billy home. Big Bill was off tour at the time, and the young couple were baffled and dismayed by the strange case.

Shirley was pregnant with her third child. Bill returned to the tour, Shirley with him. Nature clockworked her inevitable pattern and the natal day of the new child approached. In June, again when both Shirley and Bill were home, young Billy had another frightening attack. Once more his temperature shot to the boy-killing level of 106. At the hospital they packed him in ice and repeated the moot antibiotics. Antifever medication seemed to make no difference. With Shirley eight months pregnant, Bill didn't want her to spend the night in the hospital, so he asked Granny to come.

The doctor told Granny that he could do nothing, that it was touch-and-go whether Billy would make it through the night. The boy constantly complained of being cold and begged for covers with a fever of 106. The doctor had said prayer was the only defense. Granny believed utterly in the power of prayer. And she prayed. She remembered all the times she'd had to discipline Billy, and regretfully she wondered if she had been fair. Had he *really* been mischievous or was it even on those occasions this mysterious malady? "God, take care of my Billy boy. It's in your hands, God," she prayed.

The next morning about five, as Granny nodded sleepily, exhausted, young Billy sat up, smiled brightly, and said, "Hello, Granny!"

The temperature had gone.

They brought him home again. A few weeks later the pediatrician tested his gamma-globulin level and found that young Billy had pronounced gamma-globulin anemia. As the boy accompanied his parents on tour that summer, they had him checked around the country. And all diagnoses agreed: gamma-globulin anemia. The prescription was always the same: The boy would have to take maintenance doses of gamma-globulin the rest of his life.

In August of 1964, Dr. Randolph tested Shirley and the children. The allergist recommended they keep up the gamma-globulin until the program had time to operate. But he gave his prognosis that young Billy would return to normal, and that he would stay so. Less than a year later, June 1965, Granny took little Billy to see his home pediatrician, who found that he was normal. And he has remained so. The entire recovery was nearly magical. It began almost at once after the avoidance therapy started. And the cure has been permanent. No longer does he take the gamma-globulin shots. Small wonder the Caspers bless the name of Randolph.

If young Billy's cure was magical, his father's cure was equally so. We have seen how the benefits were immediate. He won the Seattle with a 265 soon after testing. It was the lowest 72-hole score that year in tournament golf. He scored four tournament wins in 1964, and amassed a total of $90,653.08. He felt better almost at once. And he had a big weight loss, a great relief to everybody. The drop in weight was due to the elimination of edema, rather than "blubber," as one galleryite dubbed it. Billy's workout period was slow. As we have seen, he had the heart trouble in Florida, and he was retested after the 1965 Western Open win. The major allergens were eliminated, disclosing the minor ones to be treated in turn. At last he was on the way up. His mental attitude improved and he blossomed into a genial, friendly man. His personality did not *change*. But instead, his true person-

ality came to the fore, since it was no longer blocked and
inhibited by poisons that upset his chemical balance.

Another member of Billy's family profoundly affected by
the program was Johnny. He had grown progressively intro-
verted, playing only intermittently with the other boys, content to be by himself, plus frequent sleepwalking, sometimes
convulsions, and often sneezing seizures of an hour's length.
But with the beginning of the avoidance therapy, John came
out of his state almost at once. And magically he returned to
normal, to the noisy, boisterous life of a happy boy.

Everyone in the household had some allergens, a few severe
and some mild. Shirley had her edema, migraine headaches,
irritated eyes, and incipient asthma. New carpeting had to be
ripped out of the boys' bedroom because the dye gave off
irritating fumes. Linda had an extreme chemical sensitivity.
But this cleared up when the Caspers changed their heating to
a hot-water system. It was certainly a good thing that Linda
was not sensitive to horse dander. She is an accomplished
horsewoman, as the more-than-a-hundred show ribbons hang-
ing in her room attest. Had she been sensitive to horses, the
Randolph program would have met a severe setback, or at
least would have created a doubting Thomas. Linda's "I don't
like elephant!" is a sharp reminder of a tempestuous scene
around the breakfast table one morning, a tale better left un-
told, though a profound argument for the veracity of Dr.
Randolph. After the avoidance therapy went into effect, Linda
became a much more tractable youngster, a sweet and affectionate young girl.

The namesake of Bob Reynolds, young son Bobby, always
had a runny nose. The elimination of sugar from his diet took
care of it. The younger the patient, the more easily corrected.
Bobby had small difficulty. Margee, a sunny-dispositioned
child only two years older, had few allergens. Most important were oatmeal, apples, and milk, the latter just like her
mother. Margee has a slight strabismus, a turning-in of the
left eye. When she is rested, this is not noticeable. When tired

or disturbed, she relaxes her concentration, and the left eye swings inward. During her testing, whenever an allergen was encountered, Margee's strabismus became pronounced and her disposition surly.

One of the most positive proofs of the value of the program came from the size changes encountered by both Billys. At seven-and-a-half, son Billy was obese and well below average at school. He wore clothing designed for a twelve-year-old. He suffered, unknowingly of course, from the gamma-globulin anemia. After the therapy, at the age of eight, Billy's grades shot up, and his clothes sizes shot down to those for an eight-year-old boy. For Bill, at the most he weighed 220, with a 40-inch waist and a 44 coat. After avoidance of his allergens, he came down to his lowest, 175, with a 34 waist and a 40 coat.

Yes, all of Bill's family were affected and improved at once with avoidance therapy. In this they are not exceptional. It happens in many families, once they become aware of it. In the Caspers' case, a predisposing factor was the intense agricultural spraying of the surrounding fields. The fields of tomato plants that Steve MacKenzie noted earlier were indirectly an almost constant menace to the entire Casper household because of the particles of chlordane spray carried in the air currents. Granny and John were particularly devastated by these. Chemical sensitivity is at once one of the most common and most virulent troubles. Billy encountered chemical allergens in Florida and Ohio. And chemical difficulties give rise to food difficulties. Both Granny and Bill have proved that if they stay free from sprays and the like, they can handle the food allergens with little difficulty.

The Casper family provided an interesting study in generations for Dr. Randolph. Granny was decidedly the most ill; Bill and Shirley were not as ill; and least ill were the children, especially Bobby and Margee. The younger the patient, the easier it is to eliminate his allergens, and the easier later to reclaim some of the foods. The older the patient, the more

complex the problem. In a few more months Granny would
have been irreversible.

Of all the persons to be mentioned in this chapter, the story
of Granny's illness and hospitalization is the most dramatic,
and potentially the most perilous.

She had moved in with the Caspers in the fall of 1963. At
Shirley and Bill's request, she assumed management of the
household while the Caspers were on tour. They all worked
together as a team. When the program started, Shirley saw
that Bill followed it religiously. Many newspaper articles
have been written about Bill's breakfasts, his buffalo steaks,
his pheasant and swordfish, etc., his "exotic diet." We have
seen that it is not a diet in the accepted sense of the word.
Shirley held the responsibility for this part of the teamwork.
As well as loving wife and companion, she was also business
manager. It would be impossible to overemphasize Shirley's
importance in this arrangement. The circumstances were most
unusual. Her husband needed her constantly on tour. Yet her
three little ones needed a mother, too. Shirley counts it fortunate that her mother was available when needed. "Mama,"
Shirley said, "we have the most beautiful relationship anybody could have." So Shirley saw to Bill, and back in Bonita
Granny saw to it that everyone at home likewise maintained
a strict regimen. For sensitive Granny, though this supervision
was an act of love, it also seemed to make her out an ogre. She
rebelled at not being able to take her rightful position as a
grandmother. Though she did her job as surrogate parent
with affectionate perfection. As *châtelaine* of the Casper
home, she has brought them together into an intact loving
unity that would have been impossible with any other person
in charge. Shirley and Bill are grateful for her firm hand at
the helm.

For a number of years—ever since her tour of duty in the
Philippines and the advent of DDT in mosquito control
around the navy base—for years Granny had suffered with
occasional infections, depressions, and periodic breakdowns.

These grew progressively worse. She underwent psychiatry, from which the most important result was the taking of numerous tranquilizers, antidepressants, and such, all of which were later found to be extremely toxic for her.

Down in the game room, an oil-burning space heater warmed Granny's part of the house. The fumes from this, mixing with oil fumes in the rest of the house, were serious inhalant allergens for her. Though at this time, Granny did not know she was chemically sensitive. So whenever she needed warmth, to get it she had to breathe slow poisons. These built up day by day.

At the end of summer, 1964, her hemoglobin had fallen dangerously low. Deep distress made her withdraw, as we have noted. She was hospitalized when Dr. Franklin suspected cancer. Shirley and Bill rushed to her side. The cancer scare turned out to be a high-grade infection, and the illness and the withdrawing became worse. She locked her door, admitting no one except her minister, who prayed. Her thoughts teased with the idea of self-destruction. Always the acme of orderliness, Granny rationalized that if only she could find a way that was not messy, she'd commit suicide. Why should she go on in constant pain, her legs and back aching, her head throbbing, pulse racing? What good was she? If only there were some way that didn't leave a mess to clean up.

Shirley tried, but could not reach her mother. Granny seemed to turn away from her loved daughter, seemed to recall and resent every negative, thoughtless thing Shirley had ever done. Shirley was helpless. But Bill got through.

Bill knocked on her door. "May I come in, Granny?"

A rush of relief flowed over her as she admitted him, though at that time she would not have acknowledged it.

"Yes, Bill," she answered quietly.

He entered and sat on the bed. In a rare gesture of affection, he held her hand. In silence. And he remained silent. It was the communion of two people dear and close who could speak from the heart, without words. And Granny's despair centered to a calm, like the eye of a hurricane the far side of which holds pent-up distress. She relaxed into life, but her thoughts were still clouded. What could she do? What good was she? But silence is therapy. For a long long time the room received the benediction of their meeting. Silence became a prayer.

Then, softly, Bill spoke. How carefully chosen each word! And spoken with just the right firmness—deferential, but authoritative. "Granny, we want to send you back to Dr. Randolph."

Tension ebbed from Granny's face and the lines of despair vanished. "All right, Bill. If I can go right now."

And prayer manifested as action.

Long distance to Chicago: The doctor would accept her only as a hospital patient, which included a fast. In the case of serious allergic illness, the fast provides the only definitive test. And Granny was seriously ill, desperately ill. So on the first available plane, Granny flew to Chicago. She took a bottle of spring water with her, cut out all the psychiatrist's medicines, and began her fast before she arrived.

Tudy, Dr. Randolph's wife and a living exemplification of the allergist's gift of life—Tudy met Granny and took her straight to the hospital. Granny felt miserable. Aches attacked her all over. Her pulse raced crazily. She was much more ill than the rest of Bill's family had been. Irritated by every little thing, cross as a bee-stung baby, Granny awaited the arrival of her allergist with a fiendish, vindictive temper.

Dr. Randolph rushed in late that evening.

"How are you?" he asked, his tone brusque.

Mentally Granny stamped her foot at the foolish question. "I feel terrible," she snapped.

Dr. Randolph rubbed his hands briskly. "Great! You're right on schedule."

And these words characterize the doctor. Brusque, all scientist, more interested in the case history than the case, yet a compassionate man who loves a joke.

The fast had started. On the third day of no-food, all thoughts of suicide left her, though pain did not. The pangs of the fast, the rapid pulses, the pains ebbing and flowing from the legs and hips—all culminated in a meal of two lobsters. The food was agreeable, and her rest was calm. Testing continued, and two weeks later Granny returned to Bonita. Much improved and ready to live, but highly sensitized, Granny had to walk a disciplined path. The path prescribed by Dr. Randolph.

As Shirley put it, "Mama, remember: you've been washed in the holy spring water."

NINE
THROUGH FAITH
"TOGETHER ALWAYS"

He was a boy. He became a youth on his way to manhood. And at last he became a man. But he was not yet a whole man. Only four of the five source streams had flowed into the making of his character. His intactness, that individualized integrity fostered by Grandpa and his mother Isabel. The love of family. A tremendous birthright of hand-to-eye coordination that resulted in an inherent ability to play golf. The program from Dr. Randolph, restoring him to health and career, and bringing euphoria to his family. These four had produced a man, an exceptional man. But not yet complete.

From earliest boyhood on, Bill searched for a father image, an unconscious though nonetheless real quest. Grandpa filled the void for a while. In an unemotional way, his father taught

107

the boy golf. Bob Reynolds came closer to the true goal than any up to that point. Others equally close were Bill Kerr and Hack Miller. Even Dr. Randolph filled the niche to some extent. This unending pursuit continued, Bill's search for the father-image he never had.

At last, when Bill's spiritual makeup was ready for it, the father-quest abandoned individuals and centered on the Church. When he found what he wanted in the Church, he was able to find it in himself. As soon as he discovered it within, he became a true father to his children, instead of just another kid for Granny to care for. He even began to be a father-image for John, who was in need of him.

It is the desire of every man to know how to live life abundantly. This comes about only through unfoldment. Unfoldment bares the true withinness. That which is within can produce evil or good, and thus it becomes a power for evil or good. The life force must be used in a balanced way. There must be a balance of the physical, the spiritual, and the mental to make up the whole man. We must embrace the spirit of life and go ahead and live it in a disciplined manner to reach fulfillment.

Granny had once said, "Bill, each man is a principality. And he must bring his principality into order, otherwise there is anarchy, and the person is at odds with himself." Bill, Granny, and Shirley all believe that the spiritual and the physical disciplines must be used together to bring about order. Order in the principality. This alone is the way to achieve the whole person.

After the 1959 U.S. Open win, Billy went to Salt Lake City, as previously noted. He played in the Utah Open, and the PGA fined him $100. Even so, it was a momentous turning point in his life. The Church of Jesus Christ of Latter-day Saints holds family life as one of its principal tenets. They say grace before meals, and the children often lead the prayers. They also have family prayers morning and evening. They have weekly family nights, when all voices are equal, child or adult, and problems are discussed. The family is an integrated unit, built as a source of strength and order. All this impressed Shirley and Bill. Especially Bill, who was inherently a family man. From this time on, the two young people seemed to gravitate toward Mormons and formed many friendships among them.

One of the strongest attractions the Church had for the Caspers was the love and respect Mormons show their children. Granny's efforts had united their own family, and Shirley and Bill wanted to learn all they could of this facet of their religious experience. The Church's beliefs on adoption were a part of this.

With careful insight it can be seen that all children are really adopted. Children are of the family of God; their entrance into mortal life is, in a sense, only a lending on God's part to the mortal parents. Thus all children are in a very real sense "adopted." The Church teaches that a child, in his preexistent life, being yet of the family of God, may have the opportunity and ability to choose the mortal parents in whose home he will receive his earthly guidance. Thus, no matter whose loins he springs from, the child will eventually reach his self-chosen father and mother, he will have finally come home. So it seemed to Shirley and Bill. And they were deeply impressed by this compassionate conviction.

There are two phases to the definition of "adoption"—the legal and the spiritual. The legal phase embraces acceptance, approval. Children are accepted, are established in the family. And they are approved, esteemed. To Shirley and Bill this seemed to crystallize all the Mormons thought about their offspring. In the spiritual phase of the definition, "adoption," when solemnized in the Temple ordinance, means a sealing into this particular unit, the Casper unit, of the family of God. It is this scriptural meaning of adoption that contains the great principles of family life and eternal relationships. A wonderful, beautiful element of the Church is the ordinance of sealing children to their parents throughout eternity. Just think, Shirley and Bill marveled, "The children, brilliant Linda, sturdy young Billy, and Bobby of the ready laugh—just think of having them throughout eternity. The children and *their* children." Visions of a whole patriarchy, sturdily marching down the centuries, hand in hand, bound close by love of family and love of God. A thrilling vision.

Prior to their friendship with the Mormons, Bill had often gone to church with Shirley. But there was something more involved than just being with his wife and children in service. A quiet acceptance of devotion showed through. An embryonic insight into things spiritual. Embryonic because it was still sleeping, though beginning to stir restlessly. Something within the man unfolded as he felt the warmth of the Mormon Church.

"When you find something good," said Bill, "you want to share it." As a famous golfer, he had more influence than an ordinary man. Because of this golf-oriented influence he was able to reach many thousands more, sharing with them the great good he had found. And this sharing has brought even greater personal growth for himself.

Before the U.S. Open playoff in 1966, when most golfers would have been resting, marshaling their strength against Palmer the next day—the night before the playoff, Bill and Shirley drove to Petaluma for a Fireside talk. They were staying at Greenbrae, about forty-five minutes from Petaluma, and arrived late. Bill showed his Vietnam slides, and they returned about midnight. Shirley prepared Bill some pork chops and sliced tomatoes. He had some good to share—and took time to do so *before the playoff!* A year before, Billy might have needed this time to rest. But now he had found a new source of strength—a spiritual strength that sustained him physically.

At the Sahara Open in 1965, Hack Miller and his wife, Barbara, brought Shirley and Bill an illustrated book, "*Meet the Mormons.*" This is a colorful and pleasing exposition of

Mormon life. Bill did not care much for reading, but the pictures told the story.

In November, Shirley and Bill went to Hawaii. With a friend they visited the site of the Mormon Temple. Jokingly, Shirley said, "Take a picture of us on the Temple steps. It's probably as close as we'll ever come to being Mormons."

But even then the Divine Presence was at work. Shirley picked up some literature. On their return flight, they read this, and the words, or the Divine Presence, or both, were effective. They decided to ask the missionaries to visit their home.

The missionaries came to bring them the Gospel. They explained that their task was not so much to convert people as it was to make the Gospel of Jesus Christ available. Then the people who were looking for the Truth could receive it.

On New Year's Day, 1966, Bill and Shirley, together with their children, were baptized into the Church of Jesus Christ of Latter-day Saints. Hack Miller officiated in the ordinance. Bill was first, then Shirley, Linda, and Billy. Bobby was too young. Afterward there was a radiance, a serenity on Bill's face never before seen.

The following day was the first Sunday of the year. At Sacrament meeting, Bill, Shirley, and the two elder children were confirmed members of the Church by the laying on of hands, and were given the gift of the Holy Ghost, and a blessing. Bobby being too young for this ordinance was given a name and a blessing.

In May, Shirley and Bill received their Patriarchal Blessing, one of the most sacred moments of their new religious life. This is a blessing given by the Stake Patriarch,* and is accompanied by fasting and prayer. To a Mormon, it is one of his greatest guidelines. He believes in it as part of his Gospel. Bill learned that he was from the "House of Ephraim," one

* A stake is a territorial division of the Church of Jesus Christ of Latter-day Saints comprising a group of wards, or congregations.

of the twelve tribes of Judah, and that he would be blessed if he maintained the standards of his Church.

Granny was happy over the Caspers' religious step. Nevertheless, it was the beginning of a schism, a fork in their lives, as she chose to walk a different path. She had deep respect for the Mormon people, and some were her dearest friends. For years she and Shirley had listened to the Sunday morning broadcasts of Richard L. Evans and the Tabernacle Choir. When the Caspers joined the Church, they matured, and Granny felt free to move away from them. She prayed for guidance. A prayer, regardless of creed, uttered with thought and feeling, secured with trust, will move mountains—the largest of which is doubt. And Granny found her answer: the children—*all* the children, little and big—were safely started on their lives' journeys, buoyed and sustained by the integrity she had imparted to them. Her job was done.

Throughout the year, Bill grew in grace and understanding. His religious wisdom and strength caused the man to advance in stature, to become mature. The first four source streams continued their outpourings of vigor. With the baptism, the fifth stream had entered his life. The man had become whole.

Today, in his Fireside talks, Bill summarizes thus:

Religion has created a formula for living. My time used to be filled with . . . golf, fishing, watching television—these were all I did. But the Gospel of Jesus Christ . . . has filled it. Golf is no longer the most important thing in my life. It is a true thing that self-discipline comes naturally from strong convictions. If as Mormons we believe that our bodies are temples of the Holy Spirit, then we take care of those bodies. This is how I overcame my weight problem, and this is why the allergies that have bothered me for years are disappearing. Shirley and I regard the family as the hearthstone of life. We hold family nights each Wednesday, without exception. All of us take part, discussing the week's experiences. Today, if someone asked me the most important thing in my life, I would immediately answer—my family and my Church.

The Church is my family. It means my family with me in the Church.

The year 1966 was drawing to a close. With the turn of the calendar, Shirley and Bill were to be married and sealed for time and eternity in the Temple at Salt Lake City. Their children were to be sealed to them, in accordance with the ordinances of the Church of Jesus Christ of Latter-day Saints.

To comprehend fully the importance of this step and the impact it has on the lives of those concerned, some discussion must be made of the Mormon concept of marriage. Above all, marriage is a sacrament, a religious act that has been solemnized by one having the authority to do so. It combines an agreement between the contracting parties and a covenant with God. In Genesis, we find, "The Lord God said, it is not good that the man should be alone; I will make him an helpmeet for him. . . . Therefore shall a man leave his father and his mother, and shall cleave unto his wife: and they shall be one flesh." By partaking in this ceremony, by officiating at it in a certain sense, God has sanctified the whole institution. He lets it be known that marriage is a natural, wholesome state, and is a major part of God's plan and purpose on and for the earth.

Marriage is more than an act or contract finalized under civil law. It is fundamentally a religious ordinance or ceremony by which a man and a woman solemnly agree to carry out the Lord's commands to make life and mortality available to His children of the spirit, and to create the possibility of their immortality and eternal life. It is more than just an agreement for the temporal existence, but includes inherently a spiritual continuation of that earthly life into the realm of exaltation in the celestial kingdom. Thus, to a Latter-Day Saint, marrige is not "until death do us part," but is a holy covenant to last "for time and all eternity." This beautiful doctrine adds depth and sacred meaning to the ceremony. And for a Latter-day Saint, this ceremony of eternal marriage must occur in a temple, and must be performed only by one having the same authority that Christ gave to Peter when he said in Matthew: "Whatsoever thou shalt bind on earth shall be bound in heaven."

Throughout the Gospels, this authority is referred to as "the keys of the kingdom of heaven." Mormons believe these Keys of Priesthood Authority to act in the name of God have been restored to the earth. In a celestial marriage, these keys open the door to that heaven. In such a marriage, there is always the duality of a life of abundance here and a life of abundance in the hereafter. And to live an abundant life in both the now and hereafter, man must love and be loved, must serve his Maker, and must exercise and bring an accounting to God for his creative talents.

Even as in all acts of faith, the true value of the deed is not to the individual, but to others. So with marriage. The true value is not to the parties concerned, but to the children begot by that marriage. The creative acts of child-conceiving, -bearing, and -rearing are the highest good that comes from the covenant of marriage. And this supreme good, as pointed out, includes the life of now and especially the life of the hereafter. Children belong to God. He is their God-father. In their pre-existence state they are His children, and are only lent to their earthly parents for earthly guidance. And this guidance includes provision for their immortality. God decrees that eternal spirit be inseparably connected to a child's rearing, so that fullness of joy may be his, with knowledge of his salvation for all time and eternity. By this it can be seen that to a Mormon, God becomes a sort of third-partner in the parent-child relationship. Bringing children into the world is part of God's plan to accomplish the immortality and eternal life of man. This is the fundament on which the Church erects its tenet of the supremacy of family life.

Christ summarized his commandments by saying that all were reduced to two commandments, the love of God and the love of fellow-man. From this, the Christian world accepts that God is Love. Since God is eternal, so therefore is Love. And thus love must extend past this earthly existence into eternity. Therefore the phrase "until death do us part" is not acceptable to members of the Church of Jesus Christ of Latter-day Saints. They aspire to be worthy of Temple marriage. The sacrament is "for time and all eternity." Thus our responsibilities to our children extend not only into the past but into the future, into "time and eternity," like a great chain whose links sweep through the centuries, forging the yesterday with the now, the now with the tomorrow.

This concept of marriage, with a perspective that includes a vast panorama of time, century upon century, from past eons that have always been to future eons that always will be —this great concatenation is the eternal belief on which the Mormon concept of marriage is founded. This gives new dignity, new meaning, adds new importance and glory to the idea of matrimony. Such marriage is primarily an act of faith, solemnized in God's presence.

"And they shall be one flesh."

These were the solemn thoughts that flowed through the minds of Shirley and Bill during the month of December. Their sacred moment was soon to come. On January 3, 1967, they would be married and sealed in the Temple, and their children would be sealed to them. For Time and all Eternity.

But before that—the holiday season. A particularly appropriate family time. Decorating for Christmas was an especially happy event. At the head of the stairs in the gathering hall, a spruce tree stood for the children. Traditionally their own tree to decorate and to show. Garlands gaily wove their bright way through the balustrade. Down in the game room, free of its oil-burner now, Granny set up her small spruce for Johnny and Margee. She kept her second family intact, though a warm part of the whole household as well. The game room acted as a living room to her wing, consisting of her bedroom, and a bedroom each for John and Margee. Guarding the integrity and individual rights of each member of the household has always been a cardinal point with her.

In the huge living room stood the family tree, a handsome spruce 12 feet tall. Joyously loaded with decorations, the tree mounted guard over hundreds of presents in their colorful wrappings. And the illuminated evergreen became a twinkling beacon of wondrous felicity.

Years before, back in the days of trailer life, Granny and Shirley had started the knitting of Christmas stockings for each child as he was born. They made them huge, optimistic as to future holiday seasons. And ten days before Christ's birthday each year, the children hang their stockings. Rather, they start the good-natured squabbling over who hangs where, and sometimes even for how long. It is a part of Christmas the world over.

One guest is always with the Caspers at Christmas. He is as much a seasonal fixture as the loaded spruce, or the Advent calendars. Manny Neikrie, from Hartford, Connecticut. To the children he is "Uncle Hartford," much loved and eagerly anticipated. A bachelor, Manny revels in the children's joy at Christmas. And the Christmas of 1966 was no exception. He had no chance to do anything else. Promptly at 5 A.M.—5 A.M.! —young Billy, John, and Bobby routed Uncle Hartford from his peaceful sleep and dragged him down the stairs. Such are the perils of avuncular visitations.

The solemn day approached and the excitement in the Casper home grew mightily. Granny was nervous. What would she do while Shirley and Bill were married and sealed in the Temple? She would not be allowed to witness the sacred rites. Neither would Johnny nor Margee. Would they leave her out altogether? But Bill and Shirley were their usual thoughtful selves, and on Christmas morning, before the children opened their gifts, the family stood breathlessly waiting while Granny opened her main present—a two-week trip to New York City to visit the Kerrs. With all details taken care of, the trek to Salt Lake City began.

The day of January 3, 1967, dawned clear but cold in Salt Lake City. Snow cast a blanket of purity over the whole countryside. To the California children, the snow was exciting, though not entirely unfamiliar. The Caspers dressed for their solemn moment. Granny was happily visiting the Kerrs in New York. Johnny and Margee would wait in the hotel. A window looked out on Temple Square, and the two children could watch the Caspers until they disappeared within the Temple itself.

Childish eyes wide in awe, little Margee gazed out on the imposing structure. Six columns of spires upon spires reached aloft. Atop the center tower in the eastern set of three, a golden angel raised a trumpet to his lips. The morning sun reflected dazzlingly yellow against the figure, sending sharp shafts of light like truth to every corner of the busy square below. Beyond the Temple, Margee could make out the rounded dome of the Tabernacle. Here, Mommy had told her, here was where the choir sang every Sunday morning. They always listened as they ate breakfast. And, oh yes, there was Brother Bill, and Sister, and Linda, and Billy, and Bobby, down there on the sidewalk. She could see them against the snow. She could always make out brother Bill; he was easy to spot. She *loved* brother Bill. She sure wished she was going with them.

This childish wish of the gregarious Margee found echo in John, though he didn't express it. And down on the sidewalk, the Casper children didn't express anything either. They walked in subdued silence, a bit timorous, awed. Their thoughts were too filled with the solemnity of the moment. They passed into the Temple.

In the Sealing Room, in solemn and sacred ceremony, Shirley and Bill were married and sealed for time and all eternity by Elder Mark E. Peterson of the Quorum of the Twelve Apostles. Then the children were brought in, to be sealed to their parents according to the prescribed order. Witnesses speak of the children "looking like white-clothed angels, wide-eyed and wondering." Just what thoughts went on in their minds is conjecture, except that once Linda said, "I kept thinking all the people were so beautiful, all in white. And how we would all be together, always, Daddy, and Mama, and Billy, and Bobby. Together always."

Out of the mouths of children: "Together always."

For Bill, it was his greatest moment.

TEN

THE U.S. OPEN—1966

Right after his baptism in 1966, Billy again went on tour. Filled with newfound faith and regained confidence, trim in figure and smiling with health, Billy soon had his first win—at San Diego. For years he had wanted to win his home-town Open. He had nearly won it the year before, but the sudden-death was won by Wes Ellis.

Billy had high hopes for the 1966 San Diego Open. On the first round, a beautiful sunny day, Tommy Aaron tied with Chris Blocker for a 65, six under par. Billy shot an undistinguished-for-him 70, though still under par. The second day, still typical California sunshine and no wind, Paul Bondeson stroked a 65, which with his 67 of the first round gave him a neat 132, a crisp ten under. Chris Blocker carded a 68, giving him a 133 for second place. Don January held steady at 134, and Billy tied with five others at 136. "I am well pleased with

my position," Billy said. And he called attention to the fact
that last year after his second round he had stood at 138, seven
behind Ellis, the eventual winner.

The third day saw some superior golf. Aaron was back on
top with a thirteen-under-par 200. He had shot a 65, 71, 64.
Don January also broke thirteen under par with most consistent rounds, 68, 66, 66—200. Zimmerman was second with
202. Rudolph and Bondeson stood at 203, and at 204, Billy
divided the niche with young Tom Weiskopf. Billy's score
was 70, 66, 68. On his eighteenth that day, Charlie Sifford
made a hole-in-one. The hole is a tough par-three of 207
yards. Sifford used a number-two iron and the ball hit about
five feet from the cup, took one bounce, and rolled straight in.
He won a $6,000 auto for his ace, his first in tournament play
and fourth in his career. Superior golf everywhere. Aaron and
January were thirteen under. Zimmerman, playing only his
second tour, had a blistering putter going, and five of his
birdie putts fell from 19, 30, 25, 20, and 10 feet. There were
48 sub-par rounds that day, and 58 players were under par
at 213 for three rounds.

Billy had a 33 going out, two under, with three short birdie
putts, and on the ninth a bogey, where his second shot found
a trap. He birdied twice on the way home, and bogeyed the
short twelfth to card a 68.

The final day was rainy and blustery. Billy's caddy, Del
Taylor, awakened grinning. It was their kind of weather. He
knew they'd win. "We hit the ball low, so I figured we'd have
the edge," Del said. Shirley saw Billy's steady eye, his ease and
quiet. He was dressed in gray on a gray day, and she liked his
looks. She noted that he was free of allergy, and she knew
he'd win. Though Billy was four behind Tommy Aaron and
Don January, the third-day leaders, he also had a hunch. The
wind from the east was strong and gusty all day, necessitating
longer-range clubs. On the third, for instance, Billy used his
driver off the tee and also for the second shot. On the tenth
hole, Casper drew even with Aaron. An old friend told Billy

he was tied for the lead, but he didn't like it and let the friend know it. Everybody kept a discreet distance after that. Billy doesn't want to know what the others are doing. All he thinks of is birdies. By the fourteenth he had the tournament wrapped up. He said that the fifth, thirteenth, and fourteenth were the key holes. On the fifth he hit a 15-inch putt that circled the cup, then dropped. On the thirteenth, which Aaron bogeyed, Billy made a 10-foot putt. He told Del, "These two holes decide it." They did. Billy knows in advance. On the fourteenth he had a birdie with a 30-foot putt. He finished with a six-under-par 64, for a total of 268, which was sixteen under par. On his final round he'd used only twenty-five putts. Seven birdies. After thirteen tries—all of the San Diego Opens!—he had finally won his home-town tournament—on buffalo steaks and sliced bananas and oranges.

Billy has always played "well within himself." This really means he thinks his way around the course. He is supercon-centrating. People think he is aloof. No. People think he is complacent, stolid. No. It is time to examine this. "I'd rather not know what others are doing," Billy has said. "All I'm interested in doing is putting as many birdies on the board as I can." The San Diego galleries are composed of numerous friends and acquaintances, but they are strangers for a time. "I don't pay much attention to the crowds except to tip my cap when they applaud a good shot," he admitted. "I get criticized for this at times."

The apparent complacency is fraudulent. He can be ruffled as well as anyone. The unconcern is superficial. He simply has it under better control than most. Some think that this causes Billy to lack "color." Conservative play, quiet, thoughtful concentration on the course—these are not the bravura dy-namics of an attention-getter. But need a golfer put on an act? Can he not play a splendid, skilled game, observing correct golf decorum as the gentleman he is, with no embellishments? Does he need pink pants with shoes to match? The color is within the man. He does not need to wrap his putter around a tree. The true golfer plays a steady, skilled game of superb nerve and concentration. Is this not color as related to golf? Is this not drama?

Many people have to rebel at some point in life. Bill has never been a rebel. It was never necessary because his integrity has always been intact. The reason for rebellion is always the establishment of integrity. Not that Bill hasn't moved forward, expanded. But rebellion has not been necessary. It has not been the prime mover.

No, a golfer's color is not flamboyant histrionics. Billy's color is inside him. It *is* the man. It is the man who can say, tongue in cheek, "Funny? You want me to be funny? Think up something funny to say and I'll say it," while even at the time his dialogue is funnier than anything you can "think up." Billy is the colorful man who on entering a locker room jammed with disgusted pros griping about the weather, or the course, or anything—Billy is the man who can come in and crack up the gathering by asking, "Is this show taped?" Popeye used to say, "I yam wot I yam and that's all wot I yam." And Billy is what he is, and that is plenty enough to be.

Some people constantly want others to improve their image. They urge this, forgetting to look in the mirror. Many have tried to persuade Billy to do this. These friends (?) argue that other golfers received so much newspaper space because their "build-ups" from publicity releases showed a better side, or more color. They wanted Billy to smile more, to be more friendly on the fairways, to wear brighter clothes. Such talk makes Billy uncomfortable, and rightly so. Any image set up by publicity releases is merely a façade. Too often that image is false. And Billy cannot tolerate falseness, especially about his game or himself. If a man is great, if a man has true humility about his greatness—and Billy has—then he needs no artificial image. He is himself, and with his integrity and intactness, if they are sufficiently stalwart to support the man, this selfness is far truer than any potpourri of adjectives poured from the smoking typewriter of a publicity hack. No one can change Billy's image. No one *need* change Billy's image. That image is his own, within the man. The purpose of this book is *not* to present an image of Billy Casper, either new or old. Instead, this book makes an honest effort to show the man as he is, with all his faults, his temperamental moments, and his moments of immortality. For Billy is among the immortals of golf. And no "image" will ever make or detract from the man.

No one knows any of the great golfers, only the newspaper cast of them. But anyone can know Billy. There he stands with his troubles and triumphs, straightforward, just, honorable. It is interesting to note, however, that this inward color of the man is beginning to surface. He used to dress most conservatively. Today his shirts are gaily striped, and complement the tones of his trousers. But never with the superficial pseudosplash of affectation. Billy doesn't have to fake.

The sportswriters had a four-under-par day with Billy's new figure, and with his "exotic diet." It is exotic, but it isn't a diet in the ordinary sense of the word. But he did lose weight with it, about 50 pounds. Bill said, "I've lost weight, but I've gained a happy life. Before, I had backaches and headaches and assorted ailments all the time. It is not true that a fat man is jolly. I was often depressed. I didn't get any fun out of life. In the eighteen months or so since I've been on the diet, I've had no aches and pains, no sicknesses, and I feel great. Everything is fun for me."

And about his game: "I'm not sure that I'm playing any better than I have before. I've almost always played well. I do know that it's easier for me to play well now than it's ever been. And I know that I'm enjoying it more than ever before."

Billy may not be considered a great driver. But he's very straight off the tee. He is a thinking golfer who walks and studies every course carefully. He commits to memory the distances and problems involved in every shot. In the morning, before Billy's arrival, his caddy, Del Taylor also walks the entire course. He knows *exactly* how many yards each club can carry for Billy. It is all charted, it is arithmetical. Sometimes Del begs Billy off a club; sometimes Billy begs Del off.

Billy never takes a club out until he's ready to use it. Once he takes it out of the bag, he's gone. If he decides to change clubs, he goes through the whole process all over again. One of the very few idiosyncrasies Billy has concerns clubs. He won't hit with a club that has a streak on it. Del must clean the streaks off several times each day. Once Billy has the club, he plays immediately. He has often wondered what the other pros thought about as they deliberated over their shots. He steps up, addresses the ball, and hits. He has always done this, even way back in Grandpa's cow pasture. It is a hallmark with him.

The relation between a golfer and his caddy is close. They are more than friends, even more than a team. It is almost as if they were *one*, not two. They say "we," but they mean a combined "I." Sometimes there is good-natured raillery. But mostly there is a silence, a serious attitude that makes the golfer the active muscle of the corporate person, but the caddy *and* the golfer together the mind. And when the relation is as deep and as full of mutual respect as Billy and Del possess, it becomes a thing of beauty.

Del left some of the big names of golf to become Billy's caddy because he felt their personalities went together. Others thought Billy a grouch in those early years. But Del says, "Never condemn a man until you know him." Once the writer had the good fortune to come upon Del as he was cleaning Billy's boots. Del did not realize anyone was nearby. He sat on the rear stoop of the Casper home, humming to himself, removing the mud. It was an act of devotion. Del was happy because he was doing something for Billy.

The caddies have great admiration for Billy. They call him "The Machine," which is a long drive from his former nickname, the "Round Man." The younger players on tour also have great admiration and respect for Billy. The latter takes time with them. He practices with the young players, not with the seasoned pros. And he never plays in a sectional tournament. He reasons that the sectional tournaments give the local pros a chance at a dollar.

Billy defended at the Bob Hope Classic in early February. At the end of the third round (out of *five*, at the Bob Hope), Billy, on Bermuda Dunes, was two shots behind the leader, Kneece, on La Quinta, though Billy had shot a 65 that day. Kneece tackled the back nine first, birdying the short seventh hole (actually his sixteenth) with a 30-foot putt. On his next-to-last hole he bogeyed with a three-putt. On his last hole, the ninth, just as he swung his driver, some golf fan on the nearby eighteenth (over the hedge) shouted. Kneece tried to keep his shot away from the lake but instead hit right into it, dunking his ball. Casper's 65 was the best round to date in this long-drawn-out tournament. He punched wedges and his high-irons tight to the flags for five of his seven birdies. The other two came on putts from 15 and 30 feet. "I putted very well," Billy said. "Only missed two greens. I was getting up to the flags with the wedge, and then down, all day." Billy's 207 was two strokes better than his score at the same position the preceding year, when he had beaten Palmer and Tommy Aaron by one stroke.

But the next day at La Quinta, which is considered two strokes harder than Bermuda Dunes, Billy fell to a 74. And at Indian Wells the last day, he shot a 70, to end tied at seventh spot with 351.

Following the Phoenix Open, where he tied for seventeenth, Bill came home for a few days rest prior to his arranged trip to the Far East. Bill wanted to visit the troops in Vietnam. He would pay his own way, considering the trip an opportunity to return to the game of golf some of the good it had given to him. His manager had scrounged around among knowledgeable people and found a Pentagon phone number which was supposed to be the correct place to call for permission to visit the troops. No one was quite sure in what office the phone rang. But Billy's manager, in the brash way that is part of a manager's equipment, dialed the number. He waited, re-hearsing his speech. A click was heard over the wire.

A rough voice said, "McNamara."

The manager gulped, then explained his request. The Secretary of Defense gave immediate consent, and Billy's trip was set up for the middle of February.

This entailed quite a bit of preparation. As usual in the Casper family, for every emergency they called on Granny. How would they find Randolph food in Vietnam and the Philippines? But Granny is a resourceful woman. As a young girl on the farm in the state of Washington, she had mastered the art of home-canning, almost a lost process in this day of packaged foods. So for about a month, Granny canned. She put up moose, elk, buffalo, and rabbit, the latter Bill's favorite. She canned pheasant and venison. And vegetables—celery, okra, carrots, and, though she isn't sure why, cauliflower and parsnips. When Shirley and Bill took off on February 18, their baggage contained many strange items, all excess. Thirteen cases. These meats, properly cooked as per the program, and packed as per home-canning—all these were to assure health and strength. The newspapers often commented on Granny's canning Billy's food.

The night before they were to take off, the house of Shirley's dressmaker burned down, destroying her complete wardrobe for the trip. But the garments were insured and, undaunted, Shirley flew into the blue yonder in eager anticipation of shopping for clothes in Hong Kong. They would fly to Honolulu, and Bill would give two exhibitions, plus a Junior-Golfer clinic, and then go on to the Philippines. Following the Philippine Open, Billy would take off for Saigon with Hack Miller, and Shirley would go to China on a shopping spree.

In Manila, Billy again conducted a free clinic for the youngsters at the Wack Wack Country Club. On the trip, Billy coupled his golf with his religion, giving Fireside talks wherever possible. In Manila he and Shirley gave a talk at the home of Pete and Maxine Grimm. When Billy moved on to Clark Air Base, he excused himself from a dinner given in his honor by the commanding general to take part in a Fireside at the home of Captain Claude Blanch. The next day, on the way from Clark to Subic Bay, in the small town of San Fernando, Shirley spotted two Americans in shirts and ties and stopped the car. The young men were Mormon missionaries on their way to an appointment. To Shirley it seemed to make the world a small place, to meet Mormons wherever she went.

Shirley accompanied Bill to many of the service hospitals. She always does this. As she looks down on the men in their beds, her thoughts dart homeward to her own boys, Billy and Bobby, and to her brother John. And always a prayer for peace comes from her heart as she smiles at the wounded. Bill is proud of her as she brings joy to the hospitalized. He says, "Shirley is the most intelligent woman I know. I couldn't get along without her. In all fields—business, public relations, as my wife—everything."

Shirley went on to Hong Kong, and Billy took off for Saigon and the Vietnam front. Almost at once he was struck by the high morale of our forces. He expected more complaining, but was agreeably surprised by the good feeling of the troops. Billy wrote of his trip, and some of the accounts were most graphic. The jungle was a constant source of amazement, especially the snakes—cobras, pythons, the deadly poisonous green bamboo snake. The Wilson Company, equipment-makers that Billy represents, donated all the balls used so that retrieving would be unnecessary. Not only was the jungle slithering with snakes and wriggling with wild animals, but Charley—the Viet Cong—lay in menacing wait. Occasionally Charley would slip past the jungle edge at night to plant a series of mines in and around the positions Casper visited. Danger was everywhere, but Billy held his clinics and gave his demonstrations, and the men cheered for more. He took many colored slides on this trip, and they enliven his Fireside chats around the country today.

The men asked so many questions, and on such diverse subjects! How had he lost so much weight? (Dr. Randolph, take a bow!) Why hadn't he won the Philippine Open? (The fumes from all that DDT spraying, the same fumes that had started Granny on her downward-circling illness, had laid Billy low.) How hot-headed was the real Tommy Bolt? (! and a couple of !!'s) Is Arnie [Palmer] a good putter? (Billy says he's tops.)

The hospital visits touched Billy most deeply. He saw hundreds of patients, some of whom had just been evacuated. One man had lost both legs at the knees. The man grinned and said, "Just as soon as they give me some equipment, I'll be out on that golf course. I may need a lesson." And Bill promised him he'd get that lesson. And he will. Another recent battle casualty was telephoning his folks. "Mom, this is sure costing somebody a whole lot," the boy said. He asked Bill to say hello to his mom and dad. Billy did. And it is one of Billy's big regrets that it didn't occur to him until later that he should have picked up the tab for that phone bill. In each case the wounded men were thinking mostly of their folks, how to protect them from unnecessary worry and suffering.

And with each new casualty, with each new courageous grin and joke, these men showed Billy the stuff Americans are made of. He said then that he felt humbled. They all expressed their gratitude for his visit. But he felt that they had given him much more than he had passed on to them.

One marine brought over a box of cookies his wife had just sent. "Would you have one, sir?"

Billy didn't want a cookie. He wanted the marine to have them. It might be a long time between boxes, so Billy smiled and shook his head.

Hurt, the marine exclaimed, "But no one's ever turned down my wife's cookies, sir."

Billy ate the cookie, and he claimed it was the best cookie he'd ever eaten.

Everyone everywhere dined Billy, and with some exotic items. Wild boar, deer, these were almost analogous to the game meat he had daily. But the Vietnamese have peculiar culinary customs. They will cook up all of a chicken except the feathers, and part of the innards. They chop it up, add a few leaves or grasses, and then cook it. Occasionally, some of the soldiers would have candy bars or canned nuts. And somehow the natives always knew this and expected to share them. After all, they shared *their* food! It was sort of a lendlease deal on an individual level. Raw meats made many of the meals memorable.

One unforgettable night, Billy watched the jets from the carrier *Ranger* take off on a bombing mission. Their tailpipes aflame, they zoomed into the sky at 3 A.M. and returned at daybreak without their eggs. He gave a golf clinic on the carrier elevator afterward, hardly expecting any guests after the strenuous flight, but the area was filled. Golfers are a long-suffering lot. He said of all the balls he dunked in the China Sea, "One thing about hitting off a moving ship, you get a hook if you shoot from portside, a slice from starboard."

Toward the end of March, Billy prepared to leave Vietnam. General Westmoreland issued an invitation to visit his headquarters. Billy was struck with the general's alertness, and with his humility. Billy also noted a Bible with several placemarkers, as if it were well read. Billy said that to him this was the sign of a right mind. The general asked Billy about his fifteen-day trip through Vietnam. Billy replied that he had visited four hospitals, four carriers, many sickbays and dispensaries, and that he had not conceived how high the morale of our fighting men could be. He had talked to thousands of men and had heard only one slight gripe. It seemed the harder a man was hit the more his bravery beamed. Field hospitals were superb. In Korea we had saved only 80 percent of our injured, but in Vietnam we were recovering 95 percent or more. Billy said that he had seen many interesting charity cases, orphans adopted by marines, and others where people had given goodies and helped with hospital aid. On the carriers he had watched pilots take off into the misty morning skies or into the dark of night, on dangerous missions. And when they came back, they would force a smile and shake their heads, admitting it had been nasty. And how glad the pilots were to talk to someone from home! How much relief it was to chat when they'd been thirty days on target, and only twelve or fourteen off.

General Westmoreland knew all this. He told Billy that he himself went every few days to the hospitals, not to boost the patients' morale but to have his own hiked. He said he'd never talked to a fighting man who'd been knocked down who hadn't actually been a morale booster to the general.

It was a memorable end to a memorable trip. Billy had been abroad for seven weeks. He'd flown evacuation missions, supply missions, reconnaissance missions, and he'd visited battle posts. He'd been fired at several times, and once he'd had to evacuate his helicopter quickly in order to avoid Charley's accuracy. He returned to the States grateful for all he'd learned about our fighting men, and grateful for the opportunity to bring them pleasure and entertainment.

Though he came back "feeling fine," the ten days he rested in his Bonita home before the Masters found him very tired. Deep-sea fishing bolstered his morale and renewed his strength somewhat. He felt he had completely recovered from his allergies, and he set out for the Masters in Augusta with high hopes. His practice round there was a three-under-par 69. But allergies are often delayed in their effects, and there had been all that spray. Billy shot 71, 75, 76, 72—294—to tie for tenth. For the second year in a row Jack Nicklaus won the Masters, and the whole pack went on to Las Vegas for the Tournament of Champions.

Palmer was defending. On the dopester sheet, Arnie and Jack were rated tops to win. At the end of the first day's play at Las Vegas, Gay Brewer and Billy were out front with two-under-par 70's. Palmer was tied for seventh with a 74, and Nicklaus and Player were far back with 76's. The big boys claimed they had a "Masters let-down." They also complained about the wiry and stubborn 6-inch rough. Billy shot five birdies and three bogeys in his opening round. The next day he shot a 71, but the third round he carded a 74. The final day he repeated his opening 70 to end with a respectable 285 that brought him third spot and $8,000. But as for a win —the Tournament of Champions was still aloof.

In June 1966, the U.S. Open was at the Olympic Club, in San Francisco. This show of shows is ordinarily a wonderful extravaganza wherein unusual plays are everyday plays, and every day has hundreds of them. But this U.S. Open was different. It settled into a two-man bout, a head-on confrontation that made screaming headlines.

The tournament opened on a typical San Francisco day— the gray cat of misty fog clinging to the Olympic course. Those teeing off in the morning could see their breaths. At the end of 36 holes, on the second day, Palmer and Casper were tied for the lead at 137. On the seventeenth that day, Billy caught a trap 62 feet from the pin. His gallery groaned, but trouble-shooting is a strong point with Billy. He chipped out with a showering blast of sand and the ball, obedient to the master's touch, nestled in the cup.

At the end of the third day, Billy was three behind. He'd had a 68-69-73. Palmer had shot a 71, a fine 66, and a par 70. Sunday, the fourth round, Billy breakfasted on ground bear. It still seemed Arnie wore a jeweled crown. At the end of the first nine, he basked in a 32, three under par and *seven* ahead of Casper, the nearest. And then Fortune took the jewels from Arnie's crown and gave them to Billy.

On the tenth, Palmer made the mistake of remembering Ben Hogan's Open record of 276, set in 1948 at the Riviera, in Los Angeles. He admitted the thought came to him that he had a chance of besting it. He began to think of beating the record instead of winning the tournament. And again he charged, followed by his army of supporters. He began to bruise the course. But Billy romanced it, wooing Lady Luck with deference. On the tenth, Arnie lost a shot, missing his putt. He bogeyed again on the thirteenth, and young son Billy received a reprimand for his rejoicing. On the par-three fifteenth, Palmer again decided to smash the course and went for the pin but ended in a bunker to the right. Billy putted a 20-footer for a two and the lead was cut to three.

The sixteenth is a long crescent-shaped blast of 604 yards. Arnie was still trying to chastise the course, which fought him back with trees and deep rough. In a tragic-comic give-and-take, Arnie lost his duel with Lady Luck and also two strokes. On the seventeenth, both golfers drove poorly, Billy sliced to the right, and Palmer pulled into deep rough on the left. Their second-shot trajectories would have crossed, and Billy was a foot short of the bunker in front of the green. But Arnie's putt came to an uphill stop just short, and Casper hit a 3-footer for par. In three holes, Billy had erased a five-stroke deficit with excellent putting under the most intense pressure an athlete can face.

On the last hole both men parred, and the unbelievable was so: Casper had come from seven behind, and the tournament would go another day.

Let us compare the previous playoff experience of each contestant. Arnie had played in twenty playoffs, winning twelve. This was his third playoff in the U.S. Open. Nicklaus beat him in 1962 at Oakmont, Pennsylvania. In 1963 he went down before Boros. Casper had been involved in only three playoffs, none in a U.S. Open. He had won one of these.

The Olympic playoff on Monday was a gargantuan duel that will stand forever among the great moments of golf. Both parred the first hole, Palmer two-putting and Billy chipping back to within 4 feet of the pin after overshooting his third. On the second hole, Palmer hit the flag with his second shot, the ball bouncing 6 feet away. His army went crazy. Then

Arnie missed his putt for a birdie. Billy's second shot bounced in a trap. He exploded out 28 feet away and sank the pill for a par. All even at two. (It must have been his breakfast of swordfish and avocado.) On the third, both players drove the green and two-putted, Palmer from 18 feet, Casper from 50 feet away. Billy responded to pressure and sank the putt for a par. All still even. On number four, Palmer dropped an 18-foot putt for a birdie. Casper reached the green in regulation and two-putted from 30 feet for a par. At the end of four: Palmer, one under; Billy, even.

On the fifth, Arnie drove in the fairway, and his pitch was 22 feet to the left of the cup. He two-putted for par. Billy's drive hit a tree on the right and dropped into the rough. His second shot was short; he pitched to within 25 feet and two-putted for a bogey: Palmer, one under; Casper, one over. On number six, both drove in the fairway, Palmer a little longer. Billy's second shot was in the left trap, but he blasted out 2 feet away and dropped in a par putt. Arnie's approach was on the collar at the back of the green, 25 feet away. He two-putted for a par. Score: Palmer still one under, Billy one over.

On the seventh, both drove into the right rough. Casper pitched to within 3 feet and sank a birdie putt. Arnie's pitch was 4 feet away and he made the birdie putt. Palmer two under, Casper even. On number eight, Billy's tee shot came down 6 feet from the pin and he sank it for a birdie two. Palmer also hit the green and two-putted from 30 feet, dropping a 4-foot second putt for a par. Palmer, two under; Casper, one under. On number nine, Palmer drove in the fairway, hit the green in regulation, and two-putted from 30 feet for par. Casper also drove in the fairway, landed his second shot on the collar at the back of the green, and three-putted from 40 feet for a bogey. At the turn: Palmer, two under; Casper, even.

On the back nine, number ten, Palmer drove in the fairway, but his second shot landed in the left trap. He blasted out 3 feet away and sank the par putt. Billy was on in regulation and

two-putted from 24 feet for a par. Score still Palmer, two
under; Casper, even. On the eleventh, both again drove in the
fairway. Casper slapped his approach shot 40 feet away and
ran it in for a birdie. Palmer hooked his approach into the left
rough, chipped to within 4 feet, but missed the putt for his
first bogey of the round. Score even at one under. On
number twelve, both were on in regulation, but Billy had a
two-putt from 50 feet for a par, and Palmer also two-putted
for a par. Still even at one under.

By this time the tension was so thick only a two-iron could
cut it. The gallery was mostly Arnie's Army, loud and unruly.
On one shot, Billy had to wait until the boisterous group left
the tee before he could drive. Billy waited, unruffled.

Weigh the moment. The giants of golf locked in a titanic
head-on battle with thousands cliffhanging over their shoulders and millions watching on TV, broadcast from the mov-
able cameras on the course and also from the Goodyear blimp
overhead. What pressure! Who would break first? At the end
of the fourth day, they had been tied at 278, just two strokes
over Hogan's all-time record. And now on the twelfth hole
they were still neck and neck, with no let-up. Arnie's Army
was growling for the kill.

That morning before going on the course, Billy had come
into the locker room and seen thirty-five or forty reporters
milling around Arnie, bantering, swapping jokes. Not one had
come over to talk to Billy. He sat waiting for Arnie. Sat alone.

And so after 84 holes that left the contestants squared off
even, Billy began his march toward golf immortality. On the
thirteenth, a distance of 191 yards, a par three, Billy's shot was
50 feet short of the pin. He ran the long putt right in for a
birdie two. Palmer's tee shot was 22 feet behind the pin and
he two-putted for a par. Score: for the first time, Billy was
in front with two under; Palmer, one under.

On number fourteen, 416 yards and a par four, Casper
drove in the fairway, came on in regulation, and two-putted
from 15 feet for par. Palmer also drove in the fairway, but was

12 yards shy on his approach. He chipped 8 feet short and missed the putt for a bogey five. Score: Casper, two under; Palmer, even.

On the fifteenth, a short 150-yard par three, Casper had a two-putt from 18 feet for a par. Palmer's tee shot caught a bunker, and he blasted out 22 feet long. A two-putt bogey went black on the scoreboard. Billy, two under; Palmer, one over.

Tension grew as they approached the sixteenth tee. It was a par-five 604-yard hole. Palmer whacked his drive into the right rough. He came back, landed short with his third, and raddled his way into a bunker on his fourth. His blastout checked 8 feet away and he missed the putt for a double-bogey seven. Groans from his Army. Billy's drive hit the rough, but he was on the green in three. He three-putted from 25 feet for a bogey six. The pace was telling on both. Score: Palmer, three over; Casper, one under.

On the seventeenth, a par four of 435 yards, both reached the green in regulation. Billy three-putted from 60 feet; Palmer's ball was at 24 feet, and he two-putted for par. He picked up one stroke, but Casper's lead was too great: Palmer, three over; Casper, even. Arnie's Army began to desert him. Cries of "Come on, Billy" filled the air. Both golfers noticed it. And Billy said to his caddy, "Hey! They're rooting for me!" What a contrast to the indifference of the reporters that morning when Billy sat alone in the locker room, waiting for Arnie.

Number eighteen is a par four of 337 yards. It was to become a rung-down curtain for Arnie's hopes in 1966. Palmer shot in the right rough. His second drew up between two traps. He chipped to 7 feet and sank his putt for a par. Billy put a star in his crown on the last hole with a perfect drive, a second shot that went 4 feet from the pin, and a dropped putt for a birdie.

Final score: Casper, 69; Palmer, 73.

Shirley cried. Del cried. And young Billy and Linda cried.

Ruth Voit, dear friend and constant galleryite, cried. Tears of joy glistened all around.

It was stupendous. The statistics alone can reveal Billy's triumph. Only fifteen sub-par scores were shot in the whole tournament. Billy had four of them. He used only 117 putts in the tournament. He one-putted 33 greens. He did not three-putt until the ninth hole of the playoff. Palmer lost six strokes to Casper in the last nine holes. And the final tie was *seven* strokes ahead of Nicklaus, the next player.

The USGA *Golf Journal* for July 1966 contains a fine summation of Billy's game, and the impact on his game of both the program and his religion: ". . . the example of Billy Casper: Mastery of a thing begins with mastery of oneself, and in being possessed by something greater than self." On the cover of the July *Golf Journal* is a touching picture of warmth and emotion: Billy and Palmer are leaving the eighteenth green after the playoff, and Casper's arm is around Arnie's shoulder. You can see he is consoling him. The commiseration was genuine.

Throughout the playoff, five-year-old Bobby stayed with the Mormon friends whom the Caspers were visiting. Several times during the tension, Bobby excused himself and ran into the bedroom. Moments later he would be back in front of the TV. Asked what he was doing, he answered, "Praying." Just before the last hole, once more Bobby left for the bedroom. He raced back in time to see his dad's winning birdie.

"Whew!" he whistled. "I'm sure glad I got in that fresher prayer!"

ELEVEN
GOLFER OF THE YEAR

The parade of wins became a montage of all the character streams that make the man. Instead of Billy's winning just because he had a certain intactness—a stubbornness, if you will which Shirley used to call "the German in him"— instead of just a single cause motivating him, now all five acted toward the common good. Improved health bolstered by his inherent ability, family love as symbolized by loyal Shirley, always hovering in the gallery—all these factors, enriched by the serenity that came from within because of his religion, began to work toward a fulfilled man.

After the stupendous U.S. Open win, Billy said, "It was a strange, unbelievable week. With nine regular holes to go I was trying hard not to finish third. Then things began to happen. I knew I played well, but I felt I was up against too much. Now I know I'll never feel down or helpless again."

One reporter asked if his recent conversion to the Mormon Church had any effect on his Open win. "There is no question but what I have received extra inner strength from this," Billy answered.

Asked if he were going to tithe his wins, Billy said, "Off the top," meaning that for the Open, his Church would receive ten percent, $2,650.

Billy is not the first golf pro to credit spiritual values with an assist. After winning his fourth Open, the mighty Hogan said, "I am very, very happy. But there is something else, too—you just can't do this without God's help."

The very next week, Billy went on to the Western Open to defend his championship at Medinah's Number 3 course, the "Monster," in Chicago. The first day, he shot all par, except for two birdies. The first was on the 175-yard par-three second. His shot with a five-iron plunked down 8 feet from the cup for a deuce. The fifth hole was 513 yards, and Billy wedged 10 feet from the pin for a birdie four. He hit the rough four times, and a trap only once. The rough was really that, and Billy said, "Once I was about an inch off the fairway, and in grass 18 inches high. I hit a six-iron with all my strength. . . . In a couple of places here the rough needs to be clipped." But despite this, he came in with a 69, two under par.

"I don't feel like I've cooled off," he said. "I feel like I'm the National Open champion, and I've got something to live up to."

However, the score was enough only for a three-way tie for second. Tommy Bolt checkreined his temper and carded a 68 to lead for the day.

On the second day, Billy again complained about the rough. "The rough is very unfair. It's a shame it was allowed to get so in such a national tournament. . . . The man who drives well but misses the fairways is penalized. The tallness of the rough graduates down the deeper you get into it, and it should be just the other way around." Billy had a 72 for 141, in second place, and only one shot ahead of Bolt and Palmer. On the third day, Casper repeated his standing of the first day, tied with three others for second.

On the fourth day, at the third hole, under 90-degree heat that punished all alike, Billy shot ahead of the pack with a 12-foot birdie putt. He missed a 5-foot putt on the sixth and bogeyed. On the eleventh he was caught in the rough near the green (that 18-inch rough he'd been griping about!), and again he took a bogey. He sank two fine birdie putts, an 8-footer on the tenth and a 6-footer on the twelfth. Final score, 69, 72, 72, 70—283, one under par, good for first place and $20,000. He led the second man, Gay Brewer, by three. Financially, it was an important tournament. For the first time he became the number-one winner on the circuit with $69,749.22. He was the first golfer to successfully defend the Western Open title since Sam Snead did it in 1949–50.

After winning $46,500 within two weeks, Billy left the tour. He decided to skip the British Open to take his family to Salt Lake City for the All-Church tournament, a worldwide golf meet for members of the Mormon Church. No fine this time; there was no regularly scheduled PGA meet. Billy's playing would be exhibition only, and he'd have leisure to get in a little fishing. For this, he took the family—Shirley, the babysitter, Linda, and the two boys.

As a family man, Bill has always deeply loved children. And they instinctively love him. And as is the way with children everywhere, they love him most when he is being a rebel, when he is acting like a little kid himself. When Granny first joined his home and accepted management of it, Bill and Shirley told her they believed a child had to master a point by concept, and learn it by precept. They wanted the Casper children to have good manners, so they asked her to eat at the table with them. Granny had been eating alone, to give her a moment's peace. However, since Granny also valued good manners, she set about fulfilling the request. She explained to the children the ways of good manners, for concept. And with her own demeanor at the table, she gave proper precept. However, the program suffered occasional setbacks at the hands of none other than Bill himself, who for a time delighted in being a big tease. He was just another boy for Granny to raise—a big "boy" but impish. He would come home from tour and, with just one word or deed, he would disrupt the politeness project. This brought a howl of delight from the children, and exasperation from Granny. Once, when the parents were off tour and taking it easy in Bonita, young Billy called out, "Daddy, throw me a piece of bread." Granny's dark blue eyes began an angry popping, much like Fourth of July sparklers. Her house of manners was about to crumble. Bill took a piece of bread and sailed it down the long table to land on Billy's plate. The children cracked up while Bill grinned sheepishly at Granny.

After the Western Open, Billy received many fan letters. Among them was one of appreciation for an autograph:

> The prime purpose of this letter is to express my deepest appreciation for the patient, polite and genuinely sincere way you signed your autograph for my nine-year-old son, who, I might add, was not in the clubhouse at the time but just another boy in the crowd following your play. You made quite an impression on him both as a golf champion and as a real gentleman.

Young Billy loves to walk the entire course and, when he can, he accompanies his father. Once a marshal cautioned caddy Del Taylor, "Don't let Billy get in the way out on the course." In a perfect though gentle squelch, Del replied, "Marshal, young Billy probably knows more about how to act on the green than you do."

One of the most touching stories about Bill's relationships with children occurred at the 1964 Carling Open, the "world's richest golf purse." At the end of the second day, Billy and Palmer were tied for second place. The next day, on the second hole, Billy's second stroke landed in the trap about 20 feet from the green. While he was studying his lie and the terrain between the ball and the cup, his caddy, a 16-year-old

Junior Golfer, raked the footprints in the trap before Billy
had a chance to shoot or to see what the caddy was doing.
After finishing the hole, Billy strode to the third tee and reported that he had called a two-stroke penalty on himself (for
raking the trap before his shot was made). The caddy didn't
know this rule and was crushed by what he had done. After
the round, Billy went to the caddy shack not to fire the
youngster, but to tell him he wanted him the next day. The
news services and TV networks cited the boy's mistake, and
when he reported for the final round he showed up hiding his
face. First prize was $35,000, and Billy ended up tied for
eighth, winning $4,033.33. Emotionally, his caddy's mistake
could have cost Billy the tournament. Financially, it did cost
him several thousand dollars. After the tournament, Billy
took the caddy with him into the locker room and spent a
half-hour telling the youngster it had not been his fault, that
it was his own, Billy's, responsibility. He added that if "Billy
Casper were perfect, he'd be shooting 65's every time he
played a round." He then gave the boy his rightful percentage
of the winnings and left on the San Diego plane.

In early July, Billy's confidence became *over*confidence.
He shilly-shallied with the ingestive part of the program, sure
that he had conquered his allergies. He temporarily forgot
that the program is not a single-action affair but a new life-
habit. Some of his earliest allergens he could have reclaimed
had he gone about it according to the prescribed plan. But
any discipline, even self-imposed, is a restraint to chafe under,
so Billy eased up. The fumes of Akron's rubber plants got to
him—despite the protestations of the Chamber of Commerce.
The fumes made his nose stop up, they irritated his lungs,
gave him terrific headaches, and in general fouled up his disposition and game. These chemical inhalants, concomitant
with his shoddily handled ingestive allergens, undid him.
Either one would have been bad, but both were severe.

Al Geiberger won the PGA with a 280. Dudley Wysong
came in second with a 284. Billy, Gene Littler, and Gary

Player tied for third, with 286. Each received $8,333.33 for his efforts. Of course, this is no small potatoes, except that after his two previous wins within a month, Billy was in the mental frame for a first. He had simply slipped in discipline. The two are integral.

He corrected his partial program lapse and immediate results followed. At the Indianapolis 500 Festival Open, all the players wore black arm ribbons in memory of Tony Lema, killed with his wife in a plane crash the week before at Lansing, Illinois. On the course, Billy carried the tournament rules in his hip pocket, since five pros had been eliminated for failure to observe the new continuous-putting rule. The defending champion, Bruce Crampton, went this route, as did Doug Ford, who had won the 500 twice, back-to-back in 1960–61.

At the close of the third day, Billy was trailing R. H. Sikes by three shots. On the eighteenth, Billy putted from the edge of the green for an eagle three shortly before Sikes broke down to a bogey six on the same hole. That one hole brought them even at nine under, a four-shot lead over Chi Chi Rodriguez.

On the final day, Billy clipped a birdie on the fifth hole, and again on the seventh he pulled feathers for a bird. He carded a 69, 70, 68, 70—277, eleven under par. Sikes started the day in the threesome ahead of Billy but ended one group behind him when Jay Hebert requested a ruling on a lie. Sikes bogeyed the fifth, and on the fifteenth his try for a bird lipped the can. He also bogeyed seventeen, scoring 69, 70, 68, and 73 for 280.

This was Billy's fourth win in 1966, and he said, "I was very happy with my putting here. The greens were hard and difficult to putt—the ball had a tendency to slip away. But I had two rounds with 31 putts and two with 32, and that's just about the way I've been putting on the tour." He waited a moment for the reporters' pencils to catch up. "The only mistake I made on the last round," he added, "was at fifteen where

I used a six-iron on the second shot—the wrong club—and trapped myself, then missed the putt for my only bogey."

He missed only two greens and four fairways on the round, and had only one three-putt green the entire four days. That came on Saturday. *One three-putt in 72 holes.*

So much has been written about Billy's putting that it seems almost impossible to offer anything new. The old adage "You drive for show, but you putt for dough" certainly seems apt in his case. In order to make this book comprehensive, some discussion of putting should be included. His tremendous records are well known. At Winged Foot he used only 114 putts, and one-putted 31 of the 72 greens. At Olympic he used only 117 putts and one-putted 33 greens. His putting triumphs have all been recorded here. But what does he think of putting?

First, Billy says, nerve control is important. Putting is a far more demanding stroke than any other—directing the ball on a definite and very narrow line. With woods or irons you're either a hooker or a fader, and you know generally where the ball will land. If you have trouble there are ways of eliminating it. You have a greater target area with the other clubs. But with the putter, there's only one place to get the ball—into a tiny hole. If you don't get it in, there's no way to make up a stroke you lose.

Rarely does Billy take more than a few seconds over any shot off the green. Even when putting, he operates with little wasted time or motion. "If you're going to miss it, miss it quickly," he jokes. And further: "I really don't understand what some of those fellows can be thinking of when they spend so much time on a shot. Each of us basically has the same checklist. Maybe it's just that I go through mine a little faster."

What are the mechanics of Billy's putt? He says, in summation, that each hand has a separate function. The left hand guides, the right hand hits. The hands should grasp the putter with equal force, but not too tightly. He uses his wrists more

than his hands and arms, developing for him a better feel of
the club head. On short putts of 10 feet or less, he taps the
ball, moving the club head through the ball and a little downward. This should leave the head just a few inches past the
ball. If the putt is longer, he brings his hands and arms into
play more. Equally important with the mechanics are the
thought-processes. He believes that you must think the ball
into the hole. And he says more putts are missed because of a
mental mistake rather than mechanical. Putting resolves into
two separate but not necessarily distinct problems: the right
speed for the ball and the right line to the hole. A golfer must
solve both; neither operates alone. It takes both speed and
line.

As Billy addresses the ball, he concentrates only on speed.
If his address is correct the problem of line is solved. He scans
the green carefully for any leaves, twigs, or other impediments.
Particularly, he notes the direction of the grain. If the grain
is against him, his putt will be slow. If it is with him, his putt
will be fast. Grain sometimes also affects the direction of
travel, causing the ball to break to one side or the other.

To address the ball, Billy first locates his right foot at right
angles to his estimated line. He takes three practice shots to
establish his rhythm, then firms up for the putt. He places the
clubhead very lightly behind the ball, just touching the grass,
then picks it up and returns it several times. "It's an up-and-
down wiggle," he says. He never raises his head to watch the
ball, but follows with his eyes until it is well on its way. And
when it's well on its way, it's on its way well.

Del Taylor has a word about Billy's putting: "We're more
cautious with the putter than anyone else. Bill doesn't believe
you should miss 3- or 4-foot putts."

But Billy is far more than golf's greatest putter. He is
strong on his woods and irons, too. Once, at a clinic, he was
asked how his tee game compared with that of Nicklaus and
Palmer. He replied that Jack would top him by 5 to 30 yards
a shot, but that Palmer's and his own game were about equal.

Comparing the drives of the two at the Olympic shows this is true. They drove almost the same distances, Palmer perhaps hitting 5 yards farther occasionally. Billy used his three wood on most of these drives.

The question of hooking or fading came up. Billy stated, "A golfer should do one or the other. These are the best ways to control the ball. The straight ball is the hardest of all to control. That's why you must decide what you want to do and then work on it." He then added, "I draw my irons and fade my woods."

He had one final bit of advice for this clinic:

Try to hit all your shots from the same position. I play mine pretty well off my left foot, chip shots and all. The old idea of moving the ball toward the right foot as you take the lesser irons is no longer the way to shape your game. Decide where you can hit the ball best, then work on it from about that position for all shots. And keep the back of the left hand going through toward the hole—very much as if the back of the left hand were actually hitting the ball.

With his Indianapolis purse of $16,400, he became the first among the pros to win four tournaments that year. He still held the year's money lead. With all five source streams working for him, Billy said, "I think my game is sharper now than it has been at any time. I feel like I'm only twenty-five years old, and I'm very happy with my putting." (He three-putted only once.)

Religion had given Billy serenity, the animals of the forests and the denizens of the sea had produced health and strength, and his biggest bothers were the chemical sprays in Florida and the rubber and other chemical fumes in Ohio. At Cleveland the week after the 500 he withdrew ill from the tournament after shooting a 65 on his last day (third round).

At the Thunderbird the next week, Billy turned in a 70 the first day, two under. The next morning he didn't feel well and skipped his usual breakfast, still carding a 68 and causing one reporter to remark that if Billy went on feeling bad he should have quite a big lead at the end of the tournament. Billy's 68 was tops and included one stroke where he wasted a shot trying to putt while simultaneously swatting at a bee on his left arm. But the third day he blew to a 76, which was followed on the final day with a 73, giving him a 287 and tying him for seventeenth.

The next week saw Billy in Hartford for the Insurance City Open as defending champion. Though he was noncommittal about it, it bothered him that he had been left off the team representing the United States in the Canada Cup Matches, to be held that year in Tokyo. The Canadian Cup doesn't necessarily have anything to do with Canada. The host nation selects the players the host would most prefer to see. Today the title "Canadian Cup" has been changed to "World Cup." And the winners of the PGA and the U.S. Open are automatically members of the team. But in 1966 Billy was disappointed at not being asked to go to Japan. His fellow golfers, too, were incensed by this omission. Especially young Dave Hill, who angrily declared, "Billy Casper's the best golfer in the world. . . . The pros should have something to say about this. . . . This team ought to be picked on merit."

Billy played consistently at the Hartford, carding a 69, 69, 64, 67—269, which tied him for third and brought $6,250 to his bulging purse. Moneywise, he still led the group.

In the last week of August, Billy went to England for the Carling World Open. Such true friends as Frances and Phillip Wilson, who handle the Piccadilly Tournament, and many Mormon friends have often made their stay in Great Britain a delight. The Carling is an unofficial tournament and does not count on PGA records, but it has a huge purse, a $35,000 first prize.

On the first day, Billy shot a par 73. Kel Nagle, an Australian, was leader for the day with a brilliant 68, five under. He had an eagle and four birdies on the back nine. He held a two-stroke lead on Peter Butler of England and a New Zealand southpaw, Bob Charles. The best the Americans could do on the first day was Jacky Cupit, Rex Baxter, and Terry Dill tied at 71, two under. Billy didn't card a birdie until Number twelve, where he sank a 30-foot putt. He had 30 putts for the round.

On the second day, Billy slumped to a 74. He said, "I'm so tired I'd like to quit." He got into real trouble on the last two holes, scoring six on each. Bert Yancey led for the day with 68 and a total of 141. On the third day it was raining and very windy. Now Billy has a wind ken. All through his career, when it's been windy, stormy, he has played better. He knows the wind as an old friend, and he knows the reaction of the ball to it. He likes rough weather. Analyzing this, one can see it is not all just strength against the elements. To be perfectly fair, we must remember that any falling rain obliterates all sprays from fairways and shrubbery. Also, with the lower temperatures of inclement weather, if any sprays are left they are less volatile. These two facts are highly important to Bill's state of health and thus indirectly important to his game. Washed-away sprays, fumes lessened because of lower volatility, his wind ken—these are some of the reasons he welcomes rough weather.

Whatever the reason, on the third day of the Carling, Casper shot a four-under 69 to be in contention. He used only 28 putts, and he had nine one-putt greens.

On the final day, Billy went out in par, carding two birdies and two bogeys. On the fifth he had a 6-foot putt, and a 30-footer on the eighth. But he trapped his approach to bogey the sixth, and he three-putted for a bogey on the seventh. Rounding the turn, Billy bogeyed the tenth when he bunkered his approach. On the thirteenth his second shot landed on the green, giving him a birdie. On the seventeenth he was short of the green on his second, but he pitched to within 5 feet, from which he sank another birdie. On the eighteenth, a par-five 531-yarder, Billy knew he had to have an eagle to tie. He hit a long drive down the middle but pulled his

second wide. Grinning and shrugging, he marched quickly to
his ball and pitched it at the pin. A big cheer rose from the
throats of the gallery. It was a 35-foot pitch. The shot
came down inches from the hole and the crowd roared. Billy
took a two-under 71, giving him 287, one shot behind the
winner, Bruce Devlin, which brought Billy second-place
money of $17,000.

Billy's biggest year was drawing to a close. The Portland—
"Caspertown"—brought him second place with a 67, 71, 67,
69—274—and $3,900. In the remaining tournaments he tied—
for twelfth at the Canadian Open, for seventh at the Sahara,
and, in Hawaii, for second. He wound up the season with a
tie for nineteenth at Houston.

Back in January, *Golf Digest* had prophesied that Billy
would be the top player of 1966. He was. This, of course,
pleased him. But when *Golf Magazine* published its awards
for the best individual club-wielders, and Billy won the
pitching-wedge award (instead of the putter), it pleased him
even more. He was leading money-winner for the year, with
$121,944.92. He was first in Ryder Cup points and in the
Vardon Trophy standings. It was his fourth year for the Vardon honor—1960, '63, '65, and '66. He had played in 319
tournaments in his twelve years as a pro. He had played in 25
in 1966, winning four, and in the money in 21 of them. He
had won a total of 33 tournaments in all, and over the years
had rung the cash register for $593,944.09! But most impor-
tant to him, he was beginning to receive the recognition and
praise from other golfers that he richly deserved. His final
kudos for 1966—his fellow-golfers gave him the highest honor
they can bestow. They elected him the PGA Player of the
Year.

Billy (at left) with Grandpa and two cousins.

Mr. and Mrs. William Adolph Casper, Grandpa and Grandma.

June 28, 1952—Billy and his bride Shirley.

At the Bing Crosby pro-amateur golf tournament, Pebble Beach, California, Billy not only won but set a new course record on January 23, 1961. (AP Wirephoto)

Victory in 1959 U.S. Open won Billy a kiss from Shirley and a coveted trophy at Mamaroneck, New York. (UPI Telephoto)

In 1963 Billy was for the second time a member of the U.S. Ryder Cup team in Great Britain, and is shown with an official and Neil Coles, a member of the British team. (Bill Mark)

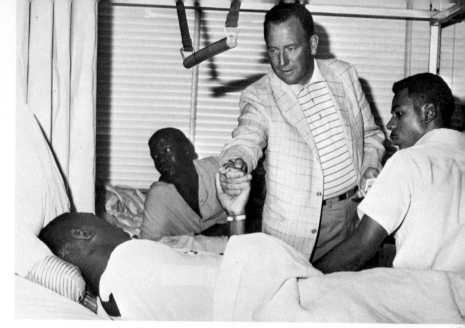

In a 1966 tour of Armed Forces installations, Billy visited hospitals and encouraged sick and wounded fighting men in Okinawa. (Official Armed Forces Photo)

He also met the legendary Green Beret soldiers in Vietnam. (Official Marine Photo)

Holding a Certificate of Appreciation from the United States Military Assistance Command Vietnam, Billy takes leave of General Westmoreland. Thanking the General on the right is Hack Miller. (Official Armed Forces Photo)

1968 found Billy in crowd-pleasing good form as he rammed home two birdies in a row at the Bob Hope Desert Golf Classic. (AP Wirephoto)

Billy delivering a Fireside talk at his church.

Serene and thoughtful, Billy looks ahead.

One of golf's most exciting events was the 1966 play-off between Billy and Arnold Palmer in San Francisco for the U.S. Open championship. (AP Wirephoto)

Family Portrait. Front: (left) Bill holds young Byron Randolph, Shirley holds baby Judy. Second row: Billy, Linda, holding young Jenny, and Bobby.

TWELVE
EARNINGS UP, WINS DOWN

In the quest for adulthood, each man wobbles a bit as he reaches a point where the boy within has to catch up. And it was so with Bill. The program was working out nicely. He was the year's top man in the golf world. Surely, he was mature and complete by now. But the boy in him had not become aware of the emerging man. Billy reached a sort of "Look, Ma! No hands" attitude toward his allergens. After all, he thought, he knew what to avoid, didn't he? Hadn't he proved it by his record? He could catch up anytime he wanted to. What did one little sugar cookie matter? He could make it up tomorrow. And so he got into trouble.

The wins stopped, and his nose stopped up. His headaches returned, and that old bugbear sinus. He was definitely in a slump. At the end of 1966, though he was high man moneywise, it was from early wins, and big ones. He was currently choking, and hating it.

The winter season of 1967 opened at San Diego, where Billy was defending the title he'd won the year before. Casper was a heavy favorite to win. His most prestigious year was behind him, and his fellow-golfers considered him as the one to beat. But they didn't know he was making hay with his health program. Full of pride over his control, he was riding gaily, his handlebars untouched.

On opening day, Young Jerry Steelsmith shot a 64, seven under par. Jerry had six birdies and an eagle. One shot behind was Randy Glover, who scored an eagle with a four-wood approach, a 25-foot putt on the tenth, and putts of 40 and 26 feet. Billy was seven back at par 71. He'd catch up tomorrow.

But he didn't. He shot a 70. Respectable golf, but not Casper golf. Steelsmith went up in a balloon to 75, but Glover stayed in the running by tying with Goalby for the lead at 132. On the third day, Billy carded a 68, for 209. The quickening pulse quickened too late, and Goalby tied the course record of 200 for 54 holes. This five-stroke lead was too much for the pack, and Bob took the top bucket the final day with a 269. Billy tied for sixth, which started his purse for the year with a slim $2,161.50. He still felt he could correct his program lapses anytime he wanted. He'd do it pretty soon. But he was enjoying eating whatever he wanted. No hands.

This belief was strengthened at the Crosby the next week. The pack roared out on three courses, all ocean-bordering and mean. At Monterey, each player tackles Cypress Point, Spyglass Hill, and the redoubtable Pebble Beach—and the fourth round is a repeat of Pebble Beach. Nicklaus led at the end of the second round. Saturday, the third round was canceled because of gale winds. Bing Crosby is always delighted when the weather acts nasty at Monterey. The weather has almost become a character in the show. The meaner it acts, the more the crooner is pleased. The horror stories about the effect of the lusty winds, and the shivering rain—all these add local color to the tournament. So the third round, delayed until Sunday, found Nicklaus leading, with Casper and Palmer chasing. Palmer was playing at Cypress Point, Nicklaus on Spyglass Hill, and Billy was beating down Pebble Beach.

Billy began Sunday four strokes behind Nicklaus. On the first hole he hit a 35-foot putt for a birdie. Again on the second hole he collected a birdie, this with a 5-footer. The rest of the nine he parred. On the turn he dropped a 3-footer for his third birdie but had to three-putt the thirteenth. On the sixteenth he tapped one in from 12 feet for another bird. And on the eighteenth, where the television camera leered at him, he missed a birdie when his 6-footer shot wide. Billy came in one under par with 215 for 54 holes. He held the lead, with Nicklaus and Palmer tied one stroke back. On Cypress Point, Arnie had mounted his clubs for a charge and carded a 67, which was seven under Jack's 74 at Spyglass Hill. Palmer grinned and said, "I know people who pick up seven strokes. It can happen. No one's immune."

On the last day, in a biting cold wind that made Der Bingle chortle, Nicklaus clobbered the final nine with a flock of birdies, five of them on the last seven holes. Three times this last day the three Mr. Big's of golf came head-on into a tie. The situation changed on fourteen of the eighteen holes. Casper held a stroke lead at the start. At the end of nine holes he had a 37; Palmer had a 36 for a tie; Jack also had a 37. On the tenth, Nicklaus and Palmer shot a par, and Billy went into a trap. Palmer was one ahead. Casper pulled even with Palmer at the eleventh by dropping a 12-foot birdie putt. Nicklaus was still one back.

The wind began lashing the course. Nicklaus's shot on the 205-yard twelfth went 6 feet past the green and about 25 feet from the cup. Jack then picked up his putter and, in his words, "just tapped it." Unbelievably, the ball went into the hole. Playing with Jack, Casper hit into the woods and went over par, losing two strokes to Nicklaus. "The twelfth was the turning point," Jack said.

But the fourteenth was important, too. Palmer, just one stroke behind at that moment, hit two fairway shots out of bounds (the second by only 1 yard) and took a nine. Nicklaus dropped a 3-foot birdie and at sixteen curled in a 55-footer. He added his fifth bird with a 17-foot putt on seventeen.

The year before, Jack had shot a nine on number eighteen, so this year he teed off with a one-iron on the 540-yard hole. He carded a par. His final score was 284, four under. Billy grabbed second spot with 72, 74, 69, 74—289—and handed over a $9,600 check to Shirley. Palmer had a 291 for $6,000.

Billy went on being diet-loose and fancy-food-free with his program. What if he did feel lousy now and then? He always knew what he'd eaten, so actually he could correct it anytime, couldn't he? He was cured, that's all.

The next week, at the Los Angeles Open, the Rancho Municipal Course was soft and balmy compared with the Waterloo of Pebble Beach, and the first day's scores showed it: thirty-eight cracked the par 71. It was a picnic. Usually, golfers don't like to criticize a course. But the leader that first day, Jacky Cupit of Longview, Texas, said, "I don't know what there is about this course, but I'm trying to make myself like it." But he had small grounds for complaint, because he shot a five-under-par 66. Eight pros tagged after him by one stroke, among them Art Wall, Julius Boros, Gay Brewer, and Doug Sanders. The three giants staggered along, Nicklaus at 69, Palmer at 70, and Billy at 72.

For Casper, everything about the tournament was topsy-turvy. His little-boy-within had not yet caught up with the whole man without, and he blamed everything but the right thing. He finished tied for sixth, again not to be taken lightly, but not a respectable score for the Open champion. He did even worse the next week, when he tied for eighth in the Bob Hope Classic. And the Phoenix was worst of all—tied for thirty-eighth spot.

After the Phoenix, Shirley returned to Bonita ahead of Bill

to prepare for their second trip to the Far East. She was worried; Bill was grumpy, irascible. Bill's friends were deeply concerned. What had happened? As before the program, Bill punished himself. He growled at everyone. "Mama," implored Shirley, "won't you talk to him?" "Can't you say something?" begged Laura Kerr. But Granny was loath. She knew Bill's trouble, and so did Shirley and Laura. You can't abandon the program. It must be a new and total way of life. Granny was about to take off for the East when Shirley made her last appeal.

"Just once more, Mama? He listens to you. It helped last time. Won't you talk to him just once more?"

Bill listens to Shirley too, thought Granny. But maybe just this time. Maybe what I say could trigger him into right action. So Granny agreed to phone Bill from Pittsburgh, as soon as he arrived home.

When she phoned she said, "Bill, you know the value of the program. You better get back on it. You still have to walk the disciplined path." And a bit later on, "You must stop saying, 'I can't putt a lick.' If you don't, that's what will happen."

Bill objected, but not vociferously. Granny had been right too many times for him to disagree. A few weeks later Bill and Shirley took off for the Philippines, Thailand, and Hong Kong. They decided Granny's canned foods were too much trouble, they'd just take their chances. Before they left, Billy received the required shots. They bothered him. He wasn't as well as on his first trip, nor was the trip as momentous. But he did visit hospitals in the Philippines, and he held clinics for the Air Force in Thailand. And ever-present Shirley, too, visited and cheered the wounded. His invisible gallery swelled as flier after flier learned to know the genuine Billy. And though for Bill the journey was a source of spiritual rejuvenation as well as joyous giving, it still entailed a sacrifice of a portion of his health. You can't take a Randolph program out to the Far East. When they returned three weeks later, they

canceled their stopover in Hawaii and came home because
they both felt poor. Three weeks in Bonita, with strict attention to the regimen, started Bill back on the routine of the
program. But nature is an exacting ruler and demands pay-
ment. At the Masters—he considers the Augusta course the
finest and most beautiful that the pros play—he shot a 294, a
number to be stated softly. At the Tournament of Champions
he used a new driver—he had wrecked his old one on the hard
courses of the Far East. During the second round, on the
fifteenth hole, Billy bull-headedly shot three balls out of
bounds from the tee and tied for eighteenth.

No doubt of it, he was allergic, and he hated to admit it.
But those who knew him could tell. It is interesting to compare how those closest to him gauge his allergenicity. As
noted earlier, his caddy says Billy is allergic when he loses his
depth-perception. Bill Kerr feels that when Billy blames a
course he is allergic. Shirley makes her decision when she
notes the lack of steadiness of his gaze. All of these are symptoms. And there are others. Whatever the cause, and no
matter whoever decides the truth of it—Billy at this time was
not shooting the game of an Open champion. And the second
Far East trip, coming concomitant with a moody state, ravaged his playing.

At Dallas he tied for tenth. At the Texas Open, in San
Antonio, he came up a bit to tie for fourth. Then at Houston
he went down again to tie for eighth. Up again at New Orleans, but only as far as a tie for fourth. Then the Colonial, a
favorite that he had won in 1964. He did a deep-six down to
tie for fifty-second! How the mighty splashes! Look, Ma!
No hands.

Billy left the tour to rest up so that he could defend his
U.S. Open championship at Baltusrol in mid-June. The first
day of that extravaganza was clammy and uncomfortable.
Young amateur Marty Fleckman startled the golf world with
a stunning three-under-par 67. Two strokes back were some
of the biggest names of golf, such as Billy, Art Wall, Gary

Player, Don January, Chi Chi Rodriguez, and Arnold Palmer. A thunderstorm halted play at Baltusrol for about half an hour. Billy lost a good chance to close the gap by one stroke on the eighteenth, where twice he stepped back from a 16-foot putt because the television cameramen were talking too loudly on a tower near the green. He rimmed the cup, then tapped in for a birdie four, carding his 69.

On the second day, Billy had a 70, Nicklaus a 67, and Palmer a 68. Fleckman had a 73 for a two-round total of 140. Palmer, leader at 137, came in for a lot of ribbing about "Hogan's record," which must have been salt on a sore wound.

On the third day the weather remained sticky, and Fleckman surprised everyone, including himself, by leading with a 69, and a 54-hole total of 209, one shot ahead of Billy, Palmer, and Nicklaus. On the fourteenth, Billy clipped a 9-foot putt to go three under par for the distance. It gave him a chance to wrap up the day. But on the fifteenth he drove deep into the rough behind a tree. He chipped back onto the fairway, and his third shot reached the green 50 feet from the cup. He got down in two putts, but he couldn't duck the bogey. On the sixteenth, a distance of 214 yards, he hit over the green and chipped 7 feet short. He missed the putt and blackened his scoreboard with another bogey. On the seventeenth tee he slammed into the left bunker. He came out badly, his ball stopping short of the drive hit by his playing partner, Bruce Devlin. Billy finally handed in a 71 for 210.

On the final day, Baltusrol lay sparkling in the New Jersey hillsides awaiting the onslaught of cars from Manhattan, a bare half-hour away. Golf was in the air and in the making. Would the amateur Fleckman manage to maintain his startling position? Would Billy be able to defend his title? Would Palmer win his fiftieth tournament? Would Jack Nicklaus's recent return to a left-to-right approach give him the advantage?

Billy bogeyed the first hole, and almost at once the Open settled into a two-way duel between Arnie and Jack. At one point, Nicklaus was within one birdie of equaling Hogan's record. It was then that he reminded himself, "Records just come." He hammered out safe pars on the fifteenth, sixteenth, and seventeenth. "Nobody should try to break a record," he said. "I'm here to win a tournament." And thus Jack avoided Palmer's mistake of the previous year at Olympic. Billy shot a 72 for 282, good for fourth place and $7,500.

At the Canadian Open early in July, Billy again became a first figure in golf. On the last day, going out on the first nine, Art Wall led by two strokes at 207. Billy was tied with Sifford and Geiberger at 210. Wall had hung to his lead doggedly for two days. Several times someone would charge at him only to be stopped by the wasteland of the seventeenth hole, a bumpy brown, practically grassless green that had the pros muttering into their putters. Young Steve Reid, a thirty-year-old part-timer on the tour, made an attack on Wall but fell on the bleak seventeenth. Dale Douglas was three under par for the round, but at the seventeenth he missed the green to the right and was stymied by a tree. He three-putted his way down. That third day, Billy shot a 71, with three birds and three bogeys.

In the final round, on the twelfth, Billy was five strokes behind. He said, "Most players would have quit right then. But I'm not made that way. I kept playing the best I could." It was the same determination that won at Olympic. And Billy began to birdie, carding five during the last fifteen holes.

Billy and Wall played together in the final threesome. Billy was two shots behind as they approached the dramatic eighteenth. Both reached the par-5 green in three. Wall was away. He studied his 20-foot putt, addressed the ball, and ran it about 5 feet past the hole. Billy stepped up, scanned the situation, then—a rare thing—he stepped back and scanned it again. At last he delicately tapped his 10-footer and it fell for a birdie. He dropped to his knees and raised his arms in exultation.

This put the pressure on Wall, a graying veteran. His putt was a 5-footer. He studied and studied. Finally, he hit and the ball rolled gently over the green. Just as it reached the cup—not more than 2 inches away—it curled. Art's shoulders slumped. He tapped his ball in for a bogey. They were tied at 279 for the 72 holes: the tournament went into a playoff.

The philosophy Billy displayed here is dominant in the man. Just as this manuscript was going to press, the writer asked him if he had any thoughts he wished to share as a culmination of his years of playing. He said, "If I can't be first, I want to be second. I want to be able to do the best I can, and at the end of the week, I want to know for myself that I have done the best I can. Never be content with mediocrity." This sums up Billy Casper better than any sentence anyone could write.

At the Canadian Open playoff, on the first hole, Billy sank a 25-foot downhill putt for a birdie. He'd had a bogey on that same hole every round of the tournament and also on a practice round. On the fourth hole, Wall evened the match with a 15-foot birdie putt. But on the next, Billy hit another fifteen-foot putt and Wall missed a short one but kept par. Both birdied the 525-yard par-five seventh hole, and both parred the eighth.

On the ninth, Casper knocked his tee shot into a trap on the fairway. He had no possibility of hitting the green with his sandy lie, but he still made par. Wall shanked a nine-iron shot into the grandstand and the ball bounced under a tree. From there, Art scraped it out into the rough, chipped, and sank a 2-foot putt for a bogey. He called it the turning point for him. "I took the club inside too quick. It was a very bad shot. I just shanked it," he said. With Billy off the green, it had been Wall's big chance of the day.

On the 435-yard tenth, Art had an easy par while Casper was off the green by about 10 feet. Billy chipped poorly, coming down 25 feet from the flag. He then proceeded to show his caliber by running in the putt. Casper felt this was the turning point for him. At the shot he was only two strokes ahead.

A string of birdies on the twelfth, thirteenth, and fifteenth

158 BILLY CASPER: WINNER

holes completely vanquished Wall. Art was in five traps, once hit a tree, again was stymied by a tree, flew one green, was out of bounds once, and finally topped a shot on the par-five fifteenth. This last hole marked an incredible performance for Wall. His drive hit a tree on the right but bounced back on the fairway. Then, using his driver, he topped the ball. He shot almost 200 yards to within 7 feet of the cup and flopped in for a birdie, one of only four. On the sixteenth, Wall birdied. On the seventeenth, they both parred. On the eighteenth, Wall's tee shot went out of bounds by a foot and he took the penalty and a bogey. Billy had six birdies without a single bogey, missed only two greens, and had eight one-putt greens. He finished with a record for the course—65, four under Wall, and six under par. Billy won $30,000, of which he gave $2,000 to his caddy.

Casper felt that his fine showing in the Canadian Open was due to his green work. He said, "It was some of my best putting in a long while." Good putting is mandatory. He feels that the most important shot, however, is the drive (this from the number-one putter!). He advises that a golfer should get his stroke polished so it is the same for all—automatic. He advises a player to eliminate all problems before he swings his club. Develop a workable mastery of the basic shots. Knowing what makes up the basic shots is elementary and mandatory. Not only how to hit each shot, but what you personally can do with each club, how far you can hit with it. As mentioned earlier, Billy and Del both walk each course on the practice round, mentally marking all fixed-position items—boulders, trees, traps, etc.

Thinking your game in this manner, you must plan each approach shot before hitting off the tee. Plan your drive so that your second shot will be an open shot, away from any course difficulty. You should take care to aim away from any hazards, traps, etc., near the green, because if you aim at the flag and miss, you are sure to meet up with trouble and a bogey or double bogey will grin at you. Also, strive for a level landing spot. This is what Billy calls "percentage golf," giving himself the best and the most opportunities (the best "percentages"). He plays for accuracy. Thus position becomes more important that distance, and for the sake of accuracy he often uses a three-wood instead of a driver off the tee. Billy goes into a tournament feeling he can win. He plays conservatively, defensively. He tries not to let bad shots bother him. As he puts it, "You never know what's going to happen tomorrow."

After the Canadian, Billy played in the 500 Festival, tying for seventh. At the PGA the next week he did not distinguish himself with a nineteenth spot. His hands still weren't on the handlebars, but they had come back for an occasional controlling touch. And he was beginning to realize what Granny had meant, that the program was an all-life thing, not just a fad.

Billy defended at the Western, but he cellared to tie for thirtieth. And as if this weren't disastrous enough, three weeks later, at the Westchester Classic, Billy submarined to a tie for fifty-ninth, totem-pole bottom! On the PGA record sheet the "win" square denoting official money won at this tournament is, of course, blank.

At the Carling World Open, in Toronto, the greens are expansive and undulating. Many golfers call the Board of Trade Country Club course a monster, but Billy found it to his liking. He always thrives under difficulties, whether it's weather or a mean, nasty course. On the first day, he apologetically turned in a 74. The second day he shone with a 68, three under. Gary Player led. As always with tournaments, the pressure began to build about the end of the second day. And by the third, Al Geiberger was leading the pack with a 209. Tied for second at 212 were Billy and Gary Player.

Going into the last day, Billy was three behind, despite a breakfast of pork chops and fresh peaches. He held the lead briefly on the back nine after shooting a one-under 35 on the front side. Geiberger was in the threesome behind Casper. Al

shot a birdie three on the thirteenth. Then Billy bogeyed the
fourteenth. At the eighteenth, Geiberger took a bite of his
peanut-butter-and-jam sandwich, then addressed the ball for a
20-foot birdie putt. The pill rolled evenly and steadily. Slowly
it teased to a stop—just 2 inches short! Al should have taken
one more bite. Billy slapped in his ball, and the match was
deadlocked at 281, three under.

For the sudden-death they replayed the fourteenth hole, a
449-yard par four. Billy drove down the fairway. Geiberger
landed in the rough to the right. Both tossed their second shots
to the left of the green, narrowly missing a pond. In fact,
though it couldn't be proved, rumor has it that both men
were saved from going into the pond by friendly spectators.
On their third shots, Geiberger chipped to within 8 feet of
the cup, Billy chipped to 3 feet. The "world's largest golf
purse" hung on the next shot. Al addressed the ball, and hit.
The ball rolled slowly, as if savoring the moment, finally coming to rest about 6 inches past the hole.

Billy scanned his 3-foot lie. $35,000 would be his for the
putting if he didn't top it, or bust it, or muff it. He placed his
feet and tapped his club in the vertical wiggle that is his hallmark. Suddenly, from a television tower above and behind
him, came loud voices that thundered out over the hushed
gallery. Billy stepped back. It was like the first round at
Baltusrol. Television men! Just as abruptly the voices ceased.
Once more Billy addressed the ball, tapped it gently. The 3-
footer rolled cleanly home, and top bucket was his.

In October, Billy went to Scotland for the Alcan "Golfer
of the Year" Tournament. First prize, $55,000, the highest
ever given in pro golf (the Carling had to revamp the title
of its advertised purse). It was an unofficial tournament,
played on St. Andrews' Old Course, the home of golf, where
for over four hundred years the game had been the life of the
countryside, where babies teethe on golf balls and every new
young one is born with a putter in his mouth. Only nineteen

golfers played the course—eleven Americans, seven Britons, and New Zealand's Bob Charles.

On the first day, Billy tied at 68 with Doug Sanders, Gardner Dickinson, and a Briton, Brian Barnes. The second day, Gay Brewer crept up and Sanders and Dickinson slid back so that Billy and Brewer were tied at 139, with young Barnes still carrying the flag for England at 141. The third day a heavy wind buffeted the course, at times reaching 45 miles an hour. The two second-round leaders stayed on top. Billy bogeyed the last two holes. On the final drop, Billy scuffed his second shot when a scorekeeper at a nearby board dropped a box of numbers just as Casper shot. "That," said Billy, "is why I look like a duffer." He came in with a 73 for a total of 212, a tie with Brewer and Barnes.

The final day marked the first time in British history that Sunday golf had been allowed. At the eleventh, Billy pulled away from Brewer, who took three putts on the hole. Both had made the turn at 37, one over par. But Gay birdied the fourteenth. Billy wedged to 4 feet on the same pin and parred. Then he birdied a 15-foot putt on the fifteenth, setting him one up. But the birdie had stoked the fire in Brewer and he finished the last three holes three-four-three, for two under, 283, a target Billy had to meet or break.

Billy had the sixteenth parred, but on the notorious seventeenth he cut the corner across the sheds that rim the fairway too close and finished in deep grass. He took his six-iron, but the ball refused to "fly" and stopped fast, 80 feet from the cup. He nearly holed the long putt, and a respectful sigh went up from the gallery. This left him with a par four to tie, a birdie to win, for the eighteenth.

His drive was a bit short and the pitch to the green was 20 feet off, with a downhill putt remaining. The difference between first and second prize was $40,000. Even at the Carling the amount had never been so big. The green looked fast, but when Billy putted the ball braked short 3 feet away. Had he birdied the hole he would have taken home $55,000. Now he had to struggle for a tie and a playoff. He addressed the ball without hesitation, and he did not miss: 283, five under par, a playoff.

The next day, in a heavy rain and wind, Brewer birdied the first hole with a 25-foot putt. Two more birdies on four and five gave him a four-stroke lead at the turn. Billy's first birdie came on the twelfth. But it was Brewer's day, and he came in four strokes ahead. Each stroke worth $10,000 to him. He took home the $55,000, and Billy the $15,000.

The following week the Piccadilly World Match Play Tournament was held at Wentworth. The meet started with some hostility. The British pros were miffed at being cut from the tournament, and some inventive scribes tried to start a feud between Brewer and Player over "the Big Three." But all this was ironed out and some taut golf resulted. Billy trounced Bruce Devlin but lost his match to Palmer, who, in the finals, took Peter Thomson in weather that would be golfable only in England.

The year 1967 was closing. It had not been the smash of 1966 as far as Billy was concerned, though oddly enough he had won more money. He won only two official tournaments, both in Canada. He had received $129,423.23, about $7,500 more than the preceding year. In 1967, Billy competed in 26 tournaments, finishing in the money 22 times. His total wins for thirteen years of pro golf added up to $723,367.32. During that time he competed in 345 tournaments and won 35. He had learned that his health program was an everyday discipline; his hands must remain securely on the handlebars of control. Even so, for the year, though his wins were down, his earnings were up.

THIRTEEN
FORE FOR THE FUTURE

The boy is a man.

The best way to demonstrate this is by contrast, a contrast between Billy's former self and the current adult. It used to be that after his round of golf at the San Diego Country Club, Billy would drop by the clubhouse to play cards. The family dinner at home would wait for him. Ordinarily, the children would have their dinner at six so their evening's activities could be accomplished by bedtime. But Bill would come in whenever it suited him. Afterward, he would go by himself into the gathering hall to watch television. He would slump onto the couch and often pull off his shirt and trousers. And he'd just sit there, with the typical glassy stare of those hypnotized by the box. It was a sad sight.

But now home life presupposes no nineteenth hole. Bill always arrives home in time for the children's dinner, and very often even before, in which case he plays ball with the boys. If he watches TV at all, it is *with the others*. He loves to stand around in the kitchen after dinner, joining in the pre-bedtime conversation of the youngsters. Occasionally he picks up a towel to dry a few pans for Connie, the maid. If honey ice cream happens to be for dessert, he stays in the kitchen for quite a while. He has a thing for honey ice cream. The number of helpings he takes is classified as top-secret information. If there is a Church job, TV can wait. The Casper home almost always has a guest or two. And if the guest happens to be Uncle Hartford, or Kendra Kerr, the beautiful young daughter of Laura and Bill—with either of these two favored friends, the rapid give-and-take conversation develops into a banter which carries such a barb that those not in the know would proclaim them mortal enemies. But this barbed banter is just a mark of Bill's special friendship.

Upstairs in the gathering hall hangs a plaque with an illuminating and relevant scriptural motto: "As for me and my house, we will serve the Lord." This paves the way for another character-revealing source of contrast—Sunday at the Caspers.

As we have seen, when Bill was a boy the most noteworthy thing about Sunday was that it was "steak day." Today, the Sabbath is set aside as God's day. If Bill is at home he goes to the Priesthood meeting at 8 A.M. Then at ten the entire family —including Anne Moffett, the "nanny" brought over from Ireland to help with the children, and Jerry Elwell, the current protégé that the Caspers are helping through college—the entire family attends Sunday school. At four in the afternoon, the whole family attends Sacrament. But their worship is not limited to the Sabbath. The weekly Home Evenings have already been mentioned. Also, Billy and Bobby attend Primary during the week, a group that interknits the children with their home and their Church, in keeping with the Mormon tenet that the hearthside is the backbone of the Church and the nation. And Tuesday nights, Linda, as well as Jerry and Anne, attend M.I.A.—Mutual Improvement Association. The

Casper's large swimming pool is quiet on Sunday. No swimming. When Billy is on tour, because of his profession, he has a special dispensation that allows him to play golf on Sundays. But he still attends as many Sunday church meetings as he can.

In the early years all he did was play golf. Shirley laid out his clothes and he put them on. Granny was both father and mother to her children, both her "big" children and the little ones. When Shirley came home, Shirley became mother and Granny was father. Billy did nothing but play golf. In the early years, B.R.—before Randolph—he was often like a prima donna denied her private dressing room. But now he is taking over the position as head of the household. When he is home, he keeps close and personal contact with every member of the household, usually having a private conversation with each on his arrival from the tour. On tour, B.R., he allowed Shirley to take care of every detail. Now Shirley stays home and Billy takes care of himself, including the cooking. He has an administrative assistant who travels with him and handles the shopping, interviews, correspondence, newsmen, etc.

Another marked difference shows in his game. He used to play in streaks. Good days would be followed by duffer days, bogeys would follow birdies. Now he is steady and there is only an occasional streakiness. His belief in goals is vital to understanding the man. This newfound steadiness stems from the day-to-day goals, and from the regular discipline of the program; additionally, and probably most important, from the serenity acquired from his religion.

He no longer punishes himself. When he accepted himself, he began to stop rejecting others, began to accept them. Until a man comes to terms with himself, the best is held back. Bill's body balance and newfound spiritual sustenance have enabled him to handle his problems. In the appendix the reader will find Dr. Randolph's words: "When a person cannot handle his daily problems, he is allergic." Bill now handles his daily problems with dexterity and competence.

One interesting facet of Bill Casper's life deserves special singling out. He loves all animals dearly. This is not a façade, nor is it an attention-getting device. It has been a strong part of his character since boyhood. When he was seven he had a pair of baby ducks. As they grew their feathers developed into the purest white. He loved them so much he couldn't leave them home when he went swimming down in the creek, so he used to take the ducks along. On one occasion he came back from his daily swim, his face wet with tears. One duck followed him, but the other he carried—dead—and his tears were very real. "He was hit by 'n ol' rattlesnake," Billy cried. "He hit him dead." But later, when his honesty caught up with him, he confessed that this duck refused to come home when called, but stayed swimming in the creek instead. In anger, Billy picked up a rock and heaved it. He caught the duck on the head, killing him (as he did the ground squirrel doing sentry duty at the cow-pasture golf course).

As a boy he took care of the farm animals. He also had his dogs, Minnie and Mike, the black German shepherd and the brown-spotted mongrel. This deep love of animals carried into his adult life. He couldn't—cannot—stand to see an animal die. Once at their Bonita home, the apron of land in front of the swimming pool, where many citrus, sapote, kumquat, and orange trees are set out—this apron was riddled with ground-squirrel holes. Bill determined to drown them out. They were a pest. They were ruining his fruit trees. He'd just put the garden hose down the hole, and—splash! They'd be no more. Wouldn't even have to bury them. He ran several hoses to various openings of the labyrinthine nest and turned on the water full force.

Sometime later, Granny came out the back door. Bill sat on the step, a covered basket of very wet scared ground squirrels beside him.

"Bill!" exclaimed Granny. "What in the world—"

He picked up one of the shivering little animals. He rubbed it dry with a huge bath towel, then peered up at Granny. "I tried," he said sheepishly. "But I couldn't do it."

Like most families, the Caspers gradually acquired their animals. Cats have a way of just appearing. But the first cat for Spanish Hill came in a different way. Young Margee, round-eyed and tender at six, came home from the stables one morning carrying a two-week-old kitten whose mother had been kicked in the head by a horse. She held the tiny shivering bundle of fur in both hands.

"Mommy," Margee said, "this kitty needs me."

She fed it with a bottle and took care of it, and today Chu Chu is a fat contented cat of three years.

The second cat just happened. One morning Poncho was there. He still is. The third cat, with beautiful long smoky hair, is called Spunky, and for the obvious reason.

Linda's horse, Big Daddy, has given her needed experience for her shows. An accomplished horsewoman, Linda takes complete care of her animal. Young Billy has a pony, Spooky, but is not the avid horseman his sister is. A third horse, Sashay, was a family gift from friends. Linda cares for all three animals.

The Casper home also has its quota of dogs. The master of the ménage is Oscar, a purebred miniature poodle. He has now reached the venerable age where the children's attentions are annoying, so he frequently takes refuge with Granny. The second dog came to the household via Bill. He and Shirley were in "Caspertown" in 1965. Shirley called home. She was a bit diffident about it. After all, Granny already had all those animals and all those kids to care for.

"Mama," Shirley said, "Bill wants to ask you something."

"Well, why doesn't he ask it?" Granny replied.

Like other kids, Bill wanted Shirley to intercede for him—but she chickened and turned the phone back.

"Granny," he stated, "there's a beautiful golden-retriever puppy up here a man wants to give me. Can we have him?"

Granny hesitated. She wondered who'd take care of the animal? "Well—" she began.

"All I have to do is name him after the man who's giving

him to me," Bill went on, as if naming the dog were the problem. "The man's nickname is Punch, so I thought we'd call
the puppy Punchy. What d'you think?"

Granny laughed. "Okay, Bill," she agreed.

And so Punchy came to Spanish Hill to serve his apprenticeship under the master, Oscar. But now Punchy's size has
dwarfed Oscar, and the golden dog has taken over the household. To Oscar, Punchy's playfulness, much like a wrestler's
massive pats, is as bothersome as the children's affectionate
embraces.

Linda brought the third dog home in her arms. A close
friend had given her the puppy.

It isn't domesticated animals alone that Bill is fond of. In the
evening, as dinner is being prepared, the coyotes in the hills
around the Casper house often come out of their dens and
begin their nocturnal baying and barking. You never see them,
but their howls split the night. On many such occasions, Bill
will stand on the small balcony off the master bedroom and
answer them. It is an amusing yet touching sight to see him
standing on the balcony, nose pointed at the pale moon rising
in the east, his mouth wide emitting barks and howls so like
the coyotes that they often answer.

One evening young Billy suggested that they get a gun and
go shoot the coyotes, that the latter were killing the neighbor's
chickens and should be shot.

But Bill caught the boy up short. "Never forget, son," he
advised. "The coyote has his right to the sun as well as we do.
There'll be no killing here."

Yes, Bill loves all animals—but he hates all flies. The writer
has seen him spend a half-hour stalking down one luckless
housefly and eventually swatting it in triumph.

With all five source streams operating at full force, Billy
drove into 1968. Actually, he'd had a two-month vacation
from golf during which he'd won the *Golf Magazine* All-
American Pitching-Wedge Award (tickling him more than
any putting award he ever won). His first tournament of the

new year was unofficial, at Buena Park, the Los Coyotes Country Club, where the Southern California Open was held. The first day, Billy hit every green in regulation and topped it by shooting an 18-foot eagle on the eighteenth to tie with two others at 68. On the second day, Al Johnston, one of the first day's leaders, duplicated his 68 and led the field, leaving Billy one stroke behind. The third day (the final day for this non-PGA tournament), Billy was in a gay mood and gave a show on the fairway. "Del," he begged, "let me go for the green with a three-wood." He shot a three-under-par 69 to win $6,000. He said, "I'm really looking forward to 1968. I feel I'm ready for the tour."

The second week of January highlighted the Bing Crosby at Monterey. Gale warnings were posted on Tuesday, but the weather surprisingly turned fair and Billy's prediction concerning his readiness proved true. He ended in a three-way sudden-death playoff with Johnny Pott and Bruce Devlin. Pott chipped in from off the green on the first extra hole to win, and Devlin and Billy tied for second. Billy won $1,800 on the Pro-Am and $7,800 on the tournament, both unofficial.

The Los Angeles Open was played at Pasadena's Brookside Course. On the second day, Billy was tied with four others for first place at 137. Stockton, George Archer, Geiberger, and Dave Marr all leveled with Billy at that spot. The weather was an important member of the cast. Chilly air blew over the course under a sun that alternately shone and hid behind darkening clouds. Finally, the day became totally overcast, and the temperature dropped to a dismal 52. The rising south wind made the back nine especially tough. But Billy, thriving on bad weather, collected five birdies, the longest with a 25-foot putt. On the difficult 458-yard twelfth he used a four-iron, his shot blistering down the fairway like a well-aimed arrow for nearly 200 yards. It lipped out of the cup but still allowed a birdie three. His only bogey came on the sixteenth hole.

On the third day, heavy overnight rains deadened the grass, making the course play two clubs longer, according to several

of the pros. On the first hole, Billy moved ahead of the pack
with a 14-foot birdie. He holed birdies of 14, 20, 30, and 7
feet. On the wicked short seventeenth he seven-ironed his ball
7 feet from the cup and dropped a birdie deuce. His score was
a three-under-par 68, giving him a third-round score of 205,
eight under. Tailing him by one stroke were Al Geiberger
and tall John Schlee. A galleryite was heard to remark, "This
can't be the same man. Casper never smiles." But Billy laughed
and cut up on the course. He was in a good mood, and ready
to live up to his name—Casper, the cut-up.

On the final day the weather relented and gave an assist.
Billy shot impeccable golf, beginning with an 8-foot birdie
putt on the first hole. On the third he tallied his first of only
two bogeys but sank putts of 10 and 5 feet on four and six
for paired birdies. The seventh had been bothering everybody,
and it caught Casper for his other bogey, a three-putt for a
five. On the back nine, Billy collected a birdie on the long
fifteenth, an easy 4-footer. He came in with a 69, winning by
three strokes with a ten-under-par 274. It was his first win at
the L.A. Open, though he'd tried thirteen times. Top money
was $20,000. The year was off with an exultant shout.

At the Bob Hope, the next week, Billy's good spirits continued. On the first day he played La Quinta. On the fifteenth
hole, a par three, Billy's drive hooked badly. His ball seemed
to disappear in the woods. He hit a provisional ball. Nearby
stood an old friend, Ruth Voit, who tells the story. When
Billy reached his first ball it was playable, though under some
bushes. He almost had to get on his hands and knees to hit it,
so that his second shot went into a sand trap. Ruth had an
instant vision of at least a six. Trembling, she watched his
third shot. The air clouded as he blasted out of the sand. The
ball hit the pin, poised a moment, then dropped in. Both Ruth
and Billy were shaking from the excitement. Billy turned to
her and laughingly said, "Routine par."

On the third day, Billy shot a 69 at Indian Wells. He would
have had a 67 and tied Palmer and Weiskopf, the leaders, ex-

cept for one of those gallery incidents. On the par-three fourth hole a spectator standing on a hill above stubbed against a rock and it slid downward. Billy was already in his backswing and the uproar caused him to shank the ball to the right for an unplayable lie. He teed up again and took a double-bogey five for the hole.

"I looked up to see what was happening," Billy said. "It sounded like a landslide. Everybody was pointing at the fellow. I felt sorry for the poor guy."

This generosity was matched by a story Weiskopf told after the tournament. He said that at one spot he was about to put his foot on the intended line of putt. It would have cost him a two-stroke penalty. But Billy saw his foot, and warned him in time.

On the fourth day, Billy played nearly perfect golf. He was two strokes behind Palmer at the opening. He pasted a 14-footer on the second hole. His second birdie came on the twelfth, a 15-foot shot. He stroked a deuce on the seventeenth from 14 feet out, and on the eighteenth he hit his third shot 1½ feet from the pin. Arnie missed a 5-footer on the eighteenth. Billy carded a 68 to lead at 279. Arnie was one behind.

Casper said, "I guess I was in the rough no more than three times, but never in trouble. I missed all the traps, hit all the greens, and fortunately had three good putts roll in." Lady Luck withdrew her smile, however, and on the final day, Billy shot a 71, dropping him into a tie for fourth.

At his home-town Open the next week, Billy came in tied for twelfth, not a distinguished score. But a distinguished comment came from the tournament. Tom Weiskopf won and afterward said, "I learned more playing two rounds with Casper than I've learned all the time I've been playing."

Billy left the tour for fishing and a rest. The white sea bass were rumored to be out at the Coronados Islands, but the boat had to be satisfied with sculpin, kelp bass, and some barracuda. Then in the latter part of February, Bill took off for his third trip to the Orient. These are important self-assigned missions to Billy, repaying the game for the good it has brought him. They are at his expense, and his religion is a constant partner. He was gone three-and-a-half weeks. He visited the Philippines, Thailand, Okinawa, and Japan. He talked with over five hundred base-hospital patients, and his invisible gallery multiplied once more.

Billy returned to the tour at Greensboro. He'd been off for almost eight weeks. His first day he shot an eight-birdie blast, five of them in a row, to score 65, five under. He was tied with Julius Boros at the top. His fellow pros marveled at how he'd returned to the tour so easily. Each day he either led or tied for the lead. On the third day he dropped back three strokes during the morning round. But two bogeys by Don January and a birdie by Billy put him back up and they were tied at 54 holes with 201. This was a two-round day, due to earlier postponements, and that afternoon Casper shot a chip-in birdie from 55 feet on the fifth hole. On the long sixth, he missed a 4-foot eagle by inches, a shot that brought him another birdie. He bogeyed number ten, and the wolves began to howl. But he "hit a very good putt of 14 feet on eleven," Billy said, and that keyed everything. On the fourteenth he clobbered a 40-footer for a birdie three, which "gave me more confidence, putting me out of reach of everyone." The birdie on the long fourteenth, and a 15-footer on the fifteenth cinched the tournament. His score—65, 67, 69, 66—267—seventeen under par. Four strokes ahead of Archer, Littler, and Nichols, tied for second. Billy's prize—$27,500.

There are two major American tournaments that Casper has never won, the Masters and the PGA. These are his goals. His five streams of strength were all pulling for him. He'd won at Los Angeles and Greensboro, and now he flew in to the Masters to greet the azaleas and the dogwood and the most beautiful course in America. He was all set to be fitted for the green coat, and on the first day he still carried the glow of earlier thoughts. Billy shot a 68 and led the pack. But on the second day he turned in a 75, which he followed with a 73 and 69 for 285: a tie for sixteenth. The Masters was still a jinx.

Billy didn't win again until the Colonial, in the middle of May. On the final day, after a breakfast of shrimp and papaya, Casper started locked with Gary Player at 207, three under par for three rounds over a 7,000-yard course. Billy grabbed the lead on the first hole, thanks to an 8-foot birdie, while Player encountered trap difficulties. On number two he again birdied, this time from 18 inches. At the fifth, Gary took a double bogey and faded from the cast. Billy took a double bogey at the par-three eighth, missing the green and then three-putting. But no one could reach him and he came in ahead of the field with 68, 71, 68, 68—275. Second was Gene Littler, five strokes behind. This five-stroke margin was Billy's biggest on tour that year, breaking his own record of four strokes at Greensboro. Casper's coin was $25,000, boosting his total take for 1968 to $104,243.54. He was now the leading money-winner for the year. It also marked the first time in golf history that a player had passed $100,000 so early in the year.

The 500 Festival Open followed a three-week vacation for fishing. On the first day, Australian Bruce Crampton sent the feathers flying with four birdies on the back nine for a four-under-par 68. Seven were tied for second at 70, among them Billy. Once more we have a demonstration of the man. He would have been tied for the lead with Crampton, except that on his third hole, Billy saw his caddy raking the trap before a shot and assessed the mandatory two-stroke penalty on himself. The same two strokes that would have brought him to a tie for first.

Crampton led again the second day with a 70 while Billy shot a 71. The third day's leader was Mike Hill, playing in only his second tour tournament. The day before he had shot a beautiful 66, placing him second. He fought sturdily until the final green, when a missed 3½-foot putt lost him the chance to tie Casper. Billy's last nine were wobbly, probably due to the humid ninety-degree heat. On the eleventh, he drove out of bounds, and on the eighteenth he was in a creek and took a penalty stroke. Both times he took bogey sixes, but he still came in with a par 36 to go with his front-nine 34, which left him two under regulation. He shot a 70, 71, 69, 70—280, eight under par. It made him the first three-time winner of the 500, his previous nods coming in 1962 and 1966. He won $20,000, bringing his total for the year to about $125,000. He had won four official tournaments and one unofficial, the Southern California Open. He led in money earned, and he had passed the $100,000 mark earlier than anyone ever had. It was going to be his year.

This is the frame of mind he brought to the U.S. Open at the Oak Hill Country Club, in Rochester, New York. In his own words: "The frame of mind is the one most important element in the game of golf."

On the first day, for his second shot—an awkward one—of the tenth hole, he chose a seven-iron. As he addressed the ball, his right foot was in a sandtrap, his left foot was in the grass. Standing at this odd angle, he shot, and a stab of pain told him he had wrenched his back muscles. He finished the round at 75 and went to his room. The pain was bad, and it was questionable whether he could continue. He had a massage, then spent an uncomfortable night. But the next day he continued to play and carded a 68. The last two days, however, he could register only a 71 and 72. Billy refuses to alibi. He had wrenched his back muscles but he was able to play. He just couldn't get the ball in the hole. He tied for ninth, eleven back of the winner, Lee Trevino.

Just before the Rochester Open, Casper experienced one of the highest emotional moments of his life. He visited the Hill of Cumorah, the site of Prophet Joseph Smith's visions a century and a half ago. Fourteen miles southwest of the golf course, Cumorah is a knoll rising about 500 feet above the Genessee Valley. Shade trees at least 250 years old set the spot aside as a haven. It is almost sacred ground for 2½ million

Mormons. Here is the fountainhead of the Church of Jesus Christ of Latter-day Saints. Here were buried the gold tablets inscribed in ancient hieroglyphic writing—Assyriac, Arabic, or Chaldaic, certified by Egyptologists of the period.

At the pre-Open dinner, Billy singled out Jim Murray, a sportswriter from the *Los Angeles Times*, and asked, "Would you like to go to Palmyra Grove with Gary Player and me tomorrow?" Murray gladly accepted.

When tomorrow arrived, Billy kept advancing the departure time. He even cut his practice round to nine holes. And at last, with Bill eagerly hurrying the two non-Mormons, they set out. On the way he told them about Joseph Smith, the country boy of fourteen who had witnessed visions. And how the angel Moroni had described for him the great civilization that had populated this continent a millennium before Columbus. How they had recorded their customs and records on gold tablets and had buried them on this hillside. From this vision, and bolstered by other visions, Joseph Smith had established the Church of Jesus Christ of Latter-day Saints, even though it led to his eventual martyrdom in Carthage, Illinois, at the hands of an armed mob daubed in war paint.

As the car approached the hallowed hill, the passengers fell silent. They stopped under the shade of a great elm tree, brave sentinel in the farmyard of the Smith family. For just a moment they hesitated before getting out. It was a moment for meditation. Billy Casper, who had received the plaudits of the world, humbly approached the hill hallowed by the visions of a country boy who possessed the equivalent of a third-grade education. As the trio moved toward the comfortable sturdy-looking farmhouse, Bill's glance darted swiftly about, absorbing, taking unto himself spiritual sustenance. When they entered the kitchen, Bill passed at once to the three-legged stove. Who knows what thoughts went on in his mind? Was he thinking clear across the country to all the evenings he had stood in his own kitchen, his children always about him? Was he thinking that he, too, in his small way, was carrying the message that Joseph Smith had heard? A cool breeze wafted through the open window, bearing the fragrance of the elms and oaks outside. Peace filled the room. A flax wheel stood in one corner. Homely items—a churn, a hurricane lamp—marked the former owner's pursuits. Bill's face was beaming as he ran his hand over the lamp. A shaft of morning sunlight came through the window, and it might have been the same sunlight that fell on young Joseph Smith's shoulders that morning so long ago. The faint rustle of leaves outside blessed the room with serenity. No one spoke. And they were still silent as they went back to their car. Bill turned and gazed long at the farmhouse nestling among the trees. He glanced up at the elm overhead, and a few rays of light filtered down. The light fell as a benediction on Bill's face as he stood there. He felt at peace, and as close to God as mortal man can ever come.

On the way back to Oak Hill, Gary Player remarked thoughtfully, "There's so much history in this country, it's a shame to know only that part of it made with thirteen clubs and a putter."

The next week, at the Canadian Open, Billy defended. But something had happened to his game. The cup was elusive, and he tied for eighth. He shot a 69, 71, 69, 71—280, six back of the winner, Bob Charles.

Throughout his professional career, Billy has grown as well as matured. The boy within has disappeared with the advent of the whole man. It is pertinent to trace what has happened to the five source streams during Billy's maturation.

The intactness, the individualized integrity so strong in his boyhood, has been calmed. But it is still as formative as ever, still under the skin, like a steel hand in a soft glove. This intactness—or call it by its other name, stubbornness—motivates Bill's actions to a great degree. It was certainly operating that day at Olympic. Only intractable stubbornness could have made Billy drive on when Palmer was seven strokes ahead.

His eye-to-hand coordination that created the natural ability to play golf has improved over the years. This is self-evident, since his game has improved. It calls for unrelenting discipline. Billy says, "It's a difficult proposition, no doubt about that— one of the few sports in which you alone are completely responsible for your play. You don't chase your opponent. He is not throwing punches at you. The ball stands still. The hole stays in its place. There is just you and that stick in your hands and everyone watching you."

Love has brought him riches of the heart. The love of his devoted wife buoys him on the fairways, even if he never acknowledges her presence. While on tour in the summer, with the children along, Billy's game picks up and his disposition becomes golden. The love and guidance and wisdom of Granny have helped form his career and have steered the destiny of the Casper family for years. And now there is a new little son, Byron Randolph. The first name is for Billy's golfing friend Byron Nelson (and the source of the middle name is obvious). Little Byron brought such sunlight into their lives that one month later the Caspers adopted two more children—Judith Kathleen and Jennifer Laura. Knowing the beliefs of Mormons concerning adoption, the reader can understand how Shirley and Bill have entered into a partnership with the Lord for the rearing of these little ones. Soon the youngsters will be sealed to their parents in the Temple. It is a rewarding act of love.

The Randolph program has returned him to health and has brought returning strength and joy to Shirley and little Billy. Today, Bill Casper is a crisp, precise person. He will answer questions directly and honestly, but he will never volunteer. Shirley says, "Bill used to come in off the tour and say that if he had to go back out again, he didn't know if he could face it." But these days he says, "I feel strong but relaxed. No aches and pains. I am able to concentrate *as I never have before.*"

And lastly, his religion has brought Bill serenity. He is calm of soul, having found his goal in life. And having found a good thing, it is like him to share it. Part of every tournament is for him the Fireside talks he gives to the local Mormon church. His God is the most important part of the man. His religion is the most important of the five sources of his character.

After the Canadian, Billy came home to celebrate his birthday, June 24. Natal days are a big thing in the Casper household, for the children especially. Margee's birthday precedes Bill's by exactly one week. He had phoned his greetings to her from Toronto, his call coming in the midst of her party. From his tone it was evident that he wished mightily he could be home for the festivities. Because Bill loves a party and he loves children, and this was both.

The twilight was silvery the night of Bill's birthday dinner, June 24. Thirty-seven years earlier, in McCullough Hospital in San Diego, he first opened his eyes. This birthday night he sat on his veranda, surrounded by his children and his loved ones, twenty-eight in all. Special among them was Keith Myres, who is also a Randolph patient. President of the San Diego South Stake, Keith has been counsel and friend to the entire family through many ups and downs.

The porch runs the entire length of the house, and in front of it is the large swimming pool. Beyond the pool a grassy esplanade stretches to where the ground falls off sharply into a grove of various fruit trees. It is this rise that gave young Billy the idea to name the house Spanish Hill. The pleasance that stretches out between the pool and hill faces nearly east, where across the valley a ragged mountain jabs the skyline. The profile of this mountain has a craggy hunk chopped out of it, looking for all the world as if some giant had taken a bite, then, dissatisfied with the taste, had spit out the rubble that streaks the hillside. This great gap catches the eye, compels the watcher to ruminate on what primeval force could have caused such a monstrous cut. The ruggedness of the gap, the barrenness of the hill below, provide and heighten a sharp contrast with the lush green valley and houses that nestle in the groves. It is a peaceful sight.

But it is not nearly so peaceful as the serenity that filled Bill's heart on his birthday night when he had his loved ones around him. He asked Jerry, young elder of the Mormon faith, to thank God for all the blessings so bountifully present. Jerry gratefully acknowledged our indebtedness to Our Maker and asked for the Lord's blessing on Billy, on the children and family surrounding, and on—the writer's gratitude is humbly acknowledged—this book.

All throughout the dinner, love abounded. Children laughed. The cats alternately approached to filch a snack and to depart hastily under the rebuke of young Bobby and Margee. Oscar and Punchy added to the hilarity and confusion with their joyful barks. At last, when no one had room for more spaghetti, Connie and Shirley cleared the tables and trays while Linda and Granny put out the dinnerware for dessert. Through the years, Shirley has matured too, and she is now mistress of her own home, with Granny a loved guest. The house bubbled with babies; in the dining room, right off the veranda, Judy and Jennifer gazed in awe at the proceedings, while big brother Byron preemptorily demanded a share in the fun. Connie brought out the ice cream, and in great pride Shirley the cake.

It was a flat cake, 3 feet long and 2 feet wide. And the decorations were like no other cake that has ever been made. They were symbolic of the moment and of the future. At the top, the words "HAPPY BIRTHDAY" trumpeted their message for all to see. Under this, in letters equally high, the word "CHAMP" stood out in proud acclaim.

HAPPY BIRTHDAY

CHAMP

Truly the words from the heart of everyone present. Equally spaced around the central message were six greens in miniature. On the flags of these indicated holes were written the names of the various tournaments Billy had won in 1968:

Los Angeles in light blue; Greensboro in pastel green; Indian-apolis in bright yellow; Colonial in warm brown; and the un-official Southern California in spanking red.

The most important green of all was in the lower right-hand corner. The flag bore a bright blue question mark. It was sig-nificant. What tournament next, Champ? And it struck the writer then that no one could ever peg Billy. He will always be the next thing that's going to happen to him. Fore for the future!

POSTSCRIPT

The question on the birthday cake icing was soon answered. At the Hartford Open in September, Billy showed the world what was next.

After the first day, Bruce Crampton led with a brilliant 65. Billy had a 68. On the second round, Billy began a sequence of what he called, "probably the best four rounds of golf I've put together." The rain was steady that second day, and Crampton complained that it affected his feel for his clubs. Despite this, Crampton posted an eagle on the par-five, 502-yard second hole. His chip shot flitted into the cup from 25 feet away. Billy claimed the rain helped his game. He took only 27 putts to card a sparkling 65 over the par-71, 6258-yard Whethersfield Country Club course. He said the rain helped hold the greens, enabling him to putt more boldly. He called it "one of my best rounds ever."

On Saturday the sun returned and Billy needed only 26 putts to whip the course. His 67 gave him a two-stroke lead over Crampton who had begun the third day with a one-stroke lead. Casper started his third-day bid with a 20-foot birdie on the first hole, and he was never in trouble.

The sun was still shining on Sunday. Billy's two-shot lead was a comfortable margin. Again he needed only 26 putts to subdue the 18 holes. He had six birds in shooting 32-34. On the par-three fifth hole, Billy's shot hit a woman fan's sweater. After a drop, he chipped in from 30 feet for a par. Final score: 68, 65, 67, 66—266. He took only 110 putts for the 72 holes and made only three bogeys. His wallet was $20,000 heavier as he won the Hartford for the third time, the first ever to do so. He finished three strokes ahead of Crampton who had a final round of 67 for a total of 269. Billy boosted his winnings to $171,431.30 for the year, and his 72-hole score was the best of the entire tour.

A few weeks later the pack went to San Francisco for the Lucky International. Again top bucket was $20,000, and Billy had confidence it was his. For several years he had held the secret goal of breaking $200,000 before the year's end. This was his first opportunity. It was typical San Francisco weather, sun shining through rain, and the fog softening all harsh lines. And Billy shot a 68, 65, 70, 66—269 to beat out Raymond Floyd for the golden pot. Casper's total for the year was now $203,769.92. He was the first player to break $200,000 in official money in one year. Nicklaus had passed that amount in combined funds the year before, but regulations didn't count both official and unofficial amounts then.

As November drew to a close, awards and notices of awards flowed in. November 23 was declared Billy Casper Day by the City and County of San Diego. Rancho Santa Fe hosted the salute. On December 18, the nation's golf writers held a banquet and tournament (if you could call it that; Billy played with every newsman present, three at a time) at La Costa, California, bestowing the title "Golfer of the Year" on him. Because of the still-steaming feud between the PGA and the touring pros, the governing body had neglected to make its annual award. But there was no one else it could go to. Billy had won six tournaments, four more than his closest competitor, Nicklaus. He had amassed a year's total of $205,168.67, the second highest sum ever collected by a professional golfer. Only Arnold Palmer has surpassed that amount.

In other fields, too, Billy's winning streak showed. In October and November the new babies were sealed in the temple to him and Shirley. His whole family was now his for time and eternity. If only Granny would bring her young ones, Johnny and Margee into the Church. He did wish they were with him, too. But then—he saw them often, and love was no less, even if they were not Mormons. On January 1, 1969, Bill was ordained to the office of a Seventy, a missionary calling of the Church of Jesus Christ of Latter-day Saints. This high appointment entitles him to do missionary work any place he is called. It is a signal honor, one he had long coveted. It is particularly meaningful in the light of his world travels.

The new year also began with a flu attack. And except for a tie for third at Los Angeles, the early tournaments were nothing spectacular for the man who had been high-money winner for the past year. He regained his health by the time of the Bob Hope Classic, in February, but so far this year he'd had no wins.

At Palm Springs, they had painted the traps red, white, and blue for color TV. General Eisenhower, ordinarily present, was ill in Walter Reed Army Hospital back in Washington. But President Nixon sent the Vice President, Spiro Agnew, to represent officialdom. On the second day, a woman approached Billy on the tenth tee and asked for his autograph for her son, Art, an enthusiastic golfer now soldiering in Vietnam. Billy obligingly complied and she wished him luck. Later, on the eleventh tee, in between bursts of rain, Billy stood shading his eyes. He wore a white cap between shots; the glare of the sun was blinding when it wasn't raining. The eleventh at Tamarisk is 207 yards, and the wind was blowing a bit toward him. He finally concluded to use a three-iron. But Del Taylor objected, feeling it called for a two-iron. Billy finally agreed. The ball took off low to the right and began drawing back toward the green. It struck the green about 30 feet from the hole, skipped twice, and rammed head-on with the flag about six inches off the ground. It plopped straight in.

As Billy approached the green, the crowd roared its appreciation. He raised his cap, as always. Andy Williams, one of the three amateurs playing in Casper's foursome, twirled his arm over his head encouraging the cheers. Billy stood looking down into the hole. "It's there all right," he said. "But I must have pulled it a little; it went in on the left side."

The woman who had asked for his autograph on the tenth tee came up. "Billy," she said, "my son Art will never believe you made a hole-in-one after I wished you luck."

Again Billy took her program and wrote: "You better believe her, Art. It's true."

Frank Beard led by two on the final round at Indian Wells. Billy was tied for second with Art Wall and Jack Montgomery. It was a day for tremendous golf. Beaman startled everyone with a course record of 62, 10 under par, carding 5 birdies and an eagle on his last nine (which were the first nine of the course). Billy quipped, "Did he play all the holes?"

On the first hole, Casper birdied to within one stroke of Beard. On four he birdied again, tying for the lead as Beard bogeyed. Billy was out front all the rest of the way. Montgomery and Wall came within one stroke after nine holes. But Montgomery bogeyed ten, and Wall bogeyed eleven. Billy wrapped up the parcel with an eagle on the fourteenth, a par-five, 478-yard hole, sinking a putt of 25 feet after a 4-wood put him on the green. Score: 71, 68, 71, 69, 66—345. The top golden nugget was $20,000 which brought his sum for the year to $30,291.76. His official total since his career began is $910,919.80. This means that sometime during 1969 Billy will pass his millionth official dollar of golf winnings. A million dollars in 15 years.

One of his latest goals to be fulfilled is also one of the most important. In late February his beloved Granny decided to bring her two small ones with her into the Church of Jesus Christ of Latter-day Saints. Bill and Shirley could hardly conceal their delight. For years they had surreptitiously planted various books and pamphlets where she might happen to pick them up. But she never appeared to notice. So her conversion was a true surprise as well as the result of much praying. On the night of March 15, 1969, Bill officiated at the sacred ordinance of baptism. As he stood in the font, his heart filled with gratitude to God for bringing this wish to fruition. Granny came into the water, her baptismal clothes flowing easily about her. He instructed her how to hold his wrist, preparatory for immersion. His gaze was gentle, his eyes were glistening. As he completed the baptism, he said her name in full as prescribed. And though the name on his lips was correct, the name in his heart was truer—*Granny*.

Billy has achieved nearly every one of his goals. But with each achievement, the way to a new summit is opened, a new goal becomes a desire. His path is always upward.

APPENDIX

THE RANDOLPH PROGRAM

Dr. Randolph's program consists of discovering a patient's allergens in order that the patient may avoid them. It is as simple as that. But the process is not simple.

According to the allergist, almost everyone has some items that throw his body chemistry off balance. The doctor prefers to use the term "chemical imbalance," rather than "allergy." This broader usage removes the condition from the simple rash, or "hives," that most people associate with the word. Allergy, then, is a condition of chemical imbalance in the body. And a person with this chemical imbalance is said to be allergic. Any person who cannot handle his daily problems, according to Dr. Randolph, is allergic. This includes most of us at one time or another.

Three kinds of allergens exist. They may be contactants, ingestants, or inhalants. People vary greatly in their sensitivity

189

to these. Some people are so extremely sensitive that under severe reaction they come near death. When a patient is so hypersensitive, he is said to be undergoing an allergic illness. Granny was one of these. So was her grandson, young Billy. Bill *could* have been one; also Granny's small son, Johnny.

The average reader perhaps will be more familiar with the contactants than with the other two. Most everyone has something that contact with brings on an irritation, such as touching a spruce or stroking a nettle. The lay person's idea of a rash is a good example of a contactant, though not all rashes come from contactants. Some, such as urticaria, are brought on by ingestants. But it is fair to record that the most familiar allergen will be something a person touches that brings out a rash, or an inflammation.

Items ingested make up a vast quantity of allergens. In today's world of substitutes, additives, preservatives, adulterants, package mixes, instant-everything—in this technological marvel of a world, the ingestants creep in undetected. If the problem of determining the areas of sensitivity was as simple as testing wheat, or corn, or beets, singly, then all the ill people could sing their way to work as blithely as the seven dwarfs. But the manufacturers add things, and they change things, or cloud the result under technical nomenclature, so not even the experts can always tell from the label just what is in the package. For instance, rye bread will often carry the designation "Made with flour," etc. A person who is wheat-sensitive could logically assume the label meant the loaf was made with rye flour, since that is the type of bread. But a great number of bakers use wheat flour as an additive. And a wheat-sensitive person would be off and climbing before anyone knew what he had eaten to cause his reaction. Also, chemical preservatives are added to most breads. And to a chemically sensitive person, any preservative is dire trouble.

Corn is an insidious foodstuff. It is used in many prepared dishes other than simple corn. It is often used in medicines, where it acts as bulk, or sometimes as binder. Some corn is even found in readymade bandages and bandage materials, though these are hardly ingestants. A highly corn-sensitive person would be extremely bothered by the bandage. Corn is perhaps one of the most common foods used in a multi-purpose manner. Thus it is often concealed. Whether this can be called an adulterant is a question only the courts can decide. It does provide serious trouble for those unfortunates who list corn among their allergens.

The most insidious of all, and perhaps the most damaging of all, are the inhalants. They are insidious because a person has already breathed them before he detects them. You cannot exhale the allergen, even if you can get rid of the air. In the case of an ingestant, you *could* spit it out without swallowing, particularly if you disliked your hostess. But with an inhalant, once it is breathed the damage is done—and the story of the polluted air over American cities is too well known to have to repeat. Smog, with its poisons, blights more than the color of the sky. To a chemically sensitive person, smog can trigger a whole syndrome of his allergic manifestations. Hay fever, that summer scourge, comes from inhaling pollen. Inhalant allergens are everywhere, are severely toxic to many, and cannot be avoided in this enlightened age of insecticides, automobile exhausts, factory chimneys, and industrial plants—not to mention backyard barbecues.

When the average lay person first hears of this program, he usually scoffs, disbelieves, sometimes even belligerently. The stronger the denial, the more suspect the protester. But the reader should remember the basic definition: allergy is a chemical imbalance. And any item that throws your body into imbalance is an allergen. The effect of an allergen on the human system results in a reaction. This reaction may show in a multitude of ways, paradoxic and individual. A cerebral reaction, certainly one of the most serious, affects the memory, the nervous system, occasionally the muscles, and the whole body euphoria. The patient will be unable to recall something he has said just recently. The brows will crease, a deep scowl

will mar the face, and the patient will show plainly considerable mental distress. An agonized, frightened look will come
in his eyes. His voice will rise, he will become extremely
irritable, and he will suspect everyone, assigning preposterous
and malicious motives to the simplest acts. Deep depression is
almost certain. Often the general malaise will be heightened by
muscular pains that seem to ebb and flow, especially through
the legs and hips. And above all, the patient will deny hotly
that he is under a reaction. In fact, this may be truthfully said
of *any*-type reaction, not just the cerebral. A patient under
reaction is a belligerent defender of what he firmly believes is
his own high state of euphoria. He is *not* undergoing a reaction, he states irritatedly. And the very anger and vehemence
with which he defends himself are sound proofs of his distress.
This "I am *not!*" is almost the first symptom, and certainly
one of the most convincing symptoms a patient demonstrates.

When Shirley first told Steve MacKenzie he probably was
allergic, Steve started to protest. He ate toast every day, and
he—Shirley caught him with the question about sneezing, or
hacking his throat. Most people make matutinal noises and
count it a standard part of awakening. Steve attributed these
to a "post-nasal drip," an offensive-sounding accusation for a
simple fact that takes a lot of unwarranted blame. But these
mild effects are the prelude to more serious symptoms in the
case of those who are extremely sensitive. The "miseries" that
rural women used to suffer, the arthritis Grandpa complains
of, the weather-predicting rheumatics of the elderly—these
are some of the common and lesser indications. On the more
serious level, alcoholism, obesity, edema, many forms of mental suffering—according to Dr. Randolph these are allergic
manifestations and could have been avoided had the patient
been tested and placed on avoidance therapy in time. Psychia-
trists are extremely interested in Dr. Randolph's statement
that 80 percent of the patients in mental institutions could
have been reclaimed had they been seen early enough. Unfor-
tunately, many medical men do not see eye-to-eye with the

Chicago allergist, despite positive and incontrovertible proof of his theories. Anyone who has witnessed his short educational film concerning the woman patient who was given (with her permission) an ingestion of beet sugar, a serious known allergen of hers—anyone who has seen the pathetic crawling on the floor, the loss of coordination, the uncontrollable mouth movements—anyone who has heard the sporadic mouthings, the suffering moans—anyone who has had this unforgettable distressing experience will never doubt the veracity of the good doctor's discoveries.

Allergens often work in strange and mysterious ways. And allergy can give rise to other illnesses. Allergy weakens the entire system in general. Then the area that is weakest undergoes attack. If a person's heart is weak or has been strained (by overweightness, for example), an allergic attack will act as a concomitant and direct assault on the cardiac system. This is the manner by which young Billy's gamma-globulin anemia became such a frightening thing. It was not directly allergen-connected, but little Billy's allergens had debilitated his entire system, and his weakest link was the first part of his defense to fall. Granny's extreme anemia and lack of iron in the blood was heightened in effect by her numerous allergens. There are cases of arthritis, multiple sclerosis, and more, where the susceptibility to allergens has made the original illness much more virulent. Piled-on allergy conditions also predispose the victim to colds, influenza, and infections of all sorts, an extension of this same thought.

Body weight thus enters the picture. The presence or absence of allergens does not cause adipose tissue *directly*, though it can cause edema. But the lowered condition of the body due to the allergens does indirectly affect weight. This is the most pronounced, most often-noted effect of Billy Casper's allergic illness. The corrective food program he follows caused a marked and tremendous loss of weight, though that was not a primary objective. Underweightness, like overweightness, can result from an advanced allergy condition or chemical imbalance. The important thing is that either of these, either under- or overweightness, is corrected when balance or even near-balance is achieved.

Grandpa influenced Billy with the dictum: "Feller's got to eat if he's gonna do his best." With such a guiding thought, most anyone would become overweight, witness Grandpa himself. This brings up the interesting question, "Are allergic manifestations inheritable?" With present-day knowledge this cannot be answered completely, though evidence exists to suggest it. As a conjecture, consider Grandpa and Billy. With Mendelian accuracy the *tendency* to obesity (at least) did alternate a generation. And it takes little imagination to see that had Grandpa known as much about allergens and their effects and reactions as Billy does, his senior years would have been much more comfortable.

One special type of reaction should be mentioned separately. With some people certain foods become so attractive that they glut past the point of satiety. Such compulsive eaters are fairly common. Ordinarily they are spotted at once by enormous girth, shortness of breath, etc. But sometimes they invert and become thinner the more they eat. Obviously this is from a glandular activity, probably the thyroid. Such addictive reaction is thus a chemical imbalance, and properly included in this discussion. The usual form finds the victim feeling low. He eats some of the food that he doesn't know he cannot tolerate, then he feels better temporarily. "See? Coffee (or tea, or chocolate, or whatever) doesn't bother me." Soon his pulse quickens, a headache develops, and he feels low again and decides just one more cup of coffee will fix him up. He drinks it. Temporary relief. And so on, as the pitiful tale repeats itself. Coffee, tea, and chocolate are among the most common, though any food could do this. An addictive reaction is insidious because it has such moments of relief.

To the sensitive, allergens are an ever-present menace, sneaking into the system via incompletely or improperly labeled packages, from barely or not at all perceptible odors, and even from as light a touch as the soft plastic covering most housewives put on an icebox dish. If it's your allergen, it will get you, and there's no escape.

There's no escape unless you avoid it. And you can avoid it only if you can identify it. Here is where Dr. Randolph is the shining knight on a white charger. This is the basis of his program.

Bill and Shirley Casper, and their children, were tested by subcutaneous injections of certain foodstuff extracts, and the extracts of certain other suspected allergens. These are prepared in a saline solution as against the orthodox phenol-based preparation. This affords the chemically sensitive patient a more accurate testing. But Dr. Randolph prefers to follow the hospital method, and this will be the one used as a demonstration here. Only the simplest part of the process will be presented.

The patient enters the hospital and immediately goes on a fast. He is placed in a chemically free environment, and is required to dress in cotton, silk, or rayon, laundered in bland soap. He is given a thorough physical examination. He must use innocuous items for his toilet. His only ingestants are spring water and Dr. Randolph's alkali-salts preparation. This latter consists of two-thirds sodium bicarbonate, and one-third potassium bicarbonate, taken as prescribed with spring water. This neutralizer aids in bringing the system into chemical balance. The fast lasts from four or five days to a week, depending on the severity of the withdrawal symptoms encountered. The fast period clears the system of all residual allergens (which quite often include tranquilizers, sleeping pills, and other medications that the patient has been taking in a futile and misdirected attack on what he thinks his illness is). At the end of the fast period, the doctor introduces specific foods one at a time, usually in large doses. These foods are what the Randolphites call "organic." Their use of the word is new, and has not yet acquired dictionary sanction. To them a food is "organic" if it has never been sprayed, if it is grown from untreated, organic seeds, and if the fertilizer used in its growth is derived from living organisms. The latter part of that definition is in the dictionary, though the first part is not. This employment of the word is so widespread now that doubtless new dictionaries will include it, particularly after the dignified delay with which lexicographers greet the appearance of a new usage. Throughout this book the word "organic" is used to mean freedom from any spraying and fertilized by organics. All foods used in testing, then, are organic. Except that when the patient undergoes the ingested chemical test, the foods are *not* organic, because that is precisely the object of the test.

Those foods that cause distress are allergens. The distress may be physiological. It may be mental. Or both. Sometimes the reactions are so severe that the procedure must be halted. Halted to clear the system of the reaction. The fast is resumed for a meal or as long as is necessary to return the patient to a cleared condition. This is accomplished through prescribed dosages of the alkali salts, mentioned earlier. Also by the administration of oxygen. In extreme cases, Dr. Randolph gives an intravenous saline injection, by which reaction can often be aborted if caught in time. Once the system is cleared, test feedings are resumed. The selected foods are representative members of various families of foods, so that future testing may follow up these avenues. At the end of the food testing the doctor tests for chemical sensitivity, both by ingestion and by subcutaneous injection.

For instance, in one case after the fast, the patient was given her choice of all she could eat of lobster, carrots, or avocados. For a food-starved patient who has been on a week's fast, this was a relatively easy choice. She ate two lobsters and had no trouble, which cleared the crustaceans, barring any paradoxic reactions. Later, after eating beef, the patient went into a violent reaction. Her heart speeded up, her breathing became very rapid, she had severe pains in her legs and back, and she became deeply depressed. Even the slightest noise irritated her beyond description. Irascible, scowling, she was a woman only her husband could love. The reaction seemed to affect her mind (she learned later that this was a typical cerebral effect). She forgot things she had just said, and did not remember discussions she had taken part in recently. This condemned all beef and any by-products of beef. Even gelatin, which is made from the hooves of cattle. Subsequent testing revealed a high sensitivity to milk. Later, she told Dr. Randolph that as a child she had to be fed goat's milk because cow's milk made her desperately ill.

The procedure after discovering the allergens is simply to avoid them. If a patient completely avoids an allergen for a year and then gradually introduces it again to his diet, say at once-a-week intervals, it is quite possible the patient may reclaim the food, and with care and sparse dosage, keep on eating it.

A very important requisite of the Randolph program is a disciplined follow-through after allergens are identified. The patient cannot rely on medications, for they are not used, except in rare instance. Even then they are specially prepared, quite often to avoid the phenol base, or corn (for the corn-sensitive) so commonly used. For a highly sensitive patient most medicines are more deadly than the malady. And for the less sensitive they can become so. Once, Granny had to undergo a gastrointestinal series. Not knowing her sensitivity, the administering physician gave her an injection to increase the flow of her digestive juices. To no avail she protested that the shot would make her ill. The doctor pooh-poohed the idea, ascribed her anxiety to feminine squeamishness, and gave the injection anyway. The shot had a phenol base. For six weeks Granny was extremely ill, with rapid pulse and breathing, depression, extreme irritability, and a general neurasthenia that made life miserable for her.

The program requires a drastic alteration in one's way of life. Everything is changed. Traveling becomes a hazard of restaurants that have never heard of organic foods and hotels that have only foam-rubber mattresses (sure evil for a chemically sensitive person). Obviously this grows extremely serious for Billy, who is constantly on tour. It is also very expensive, because all food, meats, fruits, and vegetables, must be shipped to him wherever he is. Social life undergoes almost total eclipse. No drinks—even if one were always just a moderate imbiber. Particularly hard is the effect on children, who eye other youngsters enviously at parties, where the rest can have ice cream and cake, though the allergic youngsters may not if wheat or milk is among their *bêtes noires*. Stores that carry organic foods are rare. The allergic individual quickly learns to look for carrots or potatoes that still have dirt on them. (They haven't been scrubbed with detergent.) A head of lettuce with a worm in it is a treasure of delight. (It has never been sprayed, and eliminating the worm is easy.) The seeker soon learns to haunt the health-food stores, not for the faddish foods frequently stocked, but for items made by a whole new batch of manufacturers, unfamiliar names, firms that specialize in wheat-free foods for those who need them, beefless gelatin, or margarine made without dairy products.

Kitchens in the homes of Dr. Randolph's patients are equipped with either stainless steel or ceramic utensils. Aluminum, a soft, spongelike metal, may carry over to the next food just enough of a preceding one to negate the rotation or even inject an unwanted and dreaded allergen. Randolphized homes must be all-electric. Space heating by hot water or steam is acceptable if the source of the heat is removed from the house, in a separate building. Gas is one of the most dreaded of all inhalant allergens for the chemically sensitive. Though heating all water and all space with electricity is more expensive than by other means, the additional cleanliness, and above all the vastly improved health of the patient, make an all-electric home a haven of refuge. Euphoria, even life itself, cannot be measured by dollars. Every source of inhalants must be scanned carefully, cautiously, because inhalants are insidious allergens and will creep in from rarely suspected places. Soft plastics, such as refrigerator-dish covers, the coverings for most meat sold over the counter, the wrappings for most products sold—all these soft plastics must go; they are petroleum-based and are therefore troublesome. Tinned goods may not be used, unless it is absolutely certain the tin can is unlined. The gold-colored lining that is technology's gift to canning is also based on petroleum, and for chemically sensitive patients carries danger. All water, both for cooking and drinking, must be pure spring water. Everything becomes suspect and is viewed askance. Allergens are alarmingly omnipresent for chemically sensitive people, and their lives are greatly altered.

Also the house itself undergoes considerable change. Not only must it be all-electric, but all paints must be chosen with care. Even the new so-called odorless paints are suspect, because they are made "odorless" by chemicals that may be allergens. Carpets must be cotton or wool, free from moth-preventive and rubberized backings. Dyes are particularly sneaky in their assault. Carpet padding must be pure jute fibers only. Mattresses must be pure cotton, as must the pads, sheets, pillowcases, and tickings. Sizings must be removed. Pillow fillings made from the new chemically derived materials, such as foam rubber, Dacron, etc., cannot be used. They must be feathers, down, kapok, or cotton. Draperies and window shades also must be cotton, linen, silk, or rayon. Furniture must be free of foam rubber for the chemically sensitive, and all fabric materials must be cotton, wool, or linen. Soaps must be free of detergents, and this usually entails a shift to an entirely new manufacturer. All household products—furniture polish, waxes, deodorizers, disinfectants, insecticides—must be chosen with extreme care. All spray cans are imperatively forbidden; the Freon gas used to pressure the contents is extremely toxic to many.

It may be thought that for such, living would become a

drab thing, a pale and wan existence of no joy. But such is
not the case. True, you no longer have the dubious pleasure
of stuffing yourself with eight hot dogs at a ballgame. You
cannot swill yourself under the bar with martinis. And even a
highball is usually forbidden. It may be the grape in cham-
pagne, the potato in vodka, or the grains in other hard liquors,
chemicals used in processing, or sometimes even a spray. Also,
all of the strong liquors have fermentation and thus yeast in
their process, and yeast is one of the most common allergens.
But after a few months of the program, when the taste buds
have returned to their normal function instead of being flag-
wavers for hot spices, the Randolph patient takes such a
delight in simple tastes, unadulterated and pure in presentation,
that actually his gustatory life is vastly enriched. After all,
the overlying principle is simply to return to nature, to the
way we were before technology hopped us up.

What causes some foods to be allergenic to certain patients
but not to others? No one knows. The subject of etiology is
clouded. Research and experiment are casting light through
this darkness, and Dr. Theron G. Randolph is a lonely pio-
neer. Allergens certainly seem to be inheritable. At least
people are surely born with some of their allergens. But they
may also acquire them, at least the ingestants. Constant eating
of certain food will almost always produce an allergen. Repeated exposure to inhalant chemicals also can build up allergenicity. Dr. Randolph feels that a great many Americans are
wheat-allergic due to their slice or two of toast for breakfast
each day. To avoid this he recommends rotation.

Specifically this means that four days must elapse between
ingestions of every food. If you have beef for dinner on Sunday, you can't repeat beef *in any form* until Thursday. No
hamburger for lunch. Not even gelatin. A lamb leg Monday
night, don't expect the leftover stew until Friday or later.
The reader will see at once that it will be difficult to find

twelve meals that do not have *a single repeated item*. And if the problem is compounded because some member of the family can't have this (allergen) and some don't like that, the difficulty multiplies astronomically. To mitigate this difficulty, Dr. Randolph recommends that a meal consist of only three items, or occasionally even just two. The *quantity* of each item the patient ingests is limited only by his own taut tummy. But it is advisable that the number of items not exceed three. This insures ample variety for the four days.

This is the reason for Billy Casper's exotic diet. It is no fad. It is no weight-reducer, though it did accomplish that. It is simply an effort to find *more* meats so that variety may be obtained and thus observe rotation. The meats that Steve MacKenzie helped Shirley pack in the family freezer are all variants to allow the Caspers to maintain rotation to avoid the building of allergens. Hippopotamus, elephant, elk, antelope, buffalo, reindeer, venison, bear—all expand the number of possible meals between repetitions. All are delicious. Also game meats are organic. That is, they grow up as nature intends, not shot full of injections and blanketed with insecticides. Some members of the family like antelope, some like bear. Linda rebels at elephant, though the rest love it. But that variation is encountered with any food. Granny and Shirley have learned to prepare these exotic meats with gourmet skill so that a meal in the Casper home is a culinary delight. But it isn't for the rare taste that the foods are purchased. It is for health reasons, pure and simple. And by their means, by the rotation they provide, Billy's career, his health, and the health of Granny and his elder son—all were saved.

The reader may be interested in a sample four-day menu worked out to the Caspers' requirements. Four days are chosen because this is the period of no-repeat demanded by rotation. It must be remembered that this includes everything, even to children's snacks between meals.

Breakfast	*Lunch*	*Snacks*	*Dinner*

First day:

Breakfast	Lunch	Snacks	Dinner
Broiled or poached fillet of sole, totuava *or* swordfish (in season) Grapefruit *or* berries	Tuna mixed with avocado Apricot, fresh in season or home-canned	Raisins & nuts	Ground bear in green peppers Broccoli

Second day:

Breakfast	Lunch	Snacks	Dinner
Buckwheat groats *or* oatmeal with honey *or* sorghum Stewed fresh rhubarb w/ honey *or* sorghum	Fresh pineapple & banana salad	Apples & kumquats	Broiled chicken String beans *or* spinach Natural brown rice

Third day:

Breakfast	Lunch	Snacks	Dinner
Reindeer patties w/gravy using arrowroot flour & spring water Peaches, fresh in season or home-canned	Fresh baked salmon Homemade pure rye bread *or* artichoke	Grape juice	Buffalo roast Cauliflower Baked yam

Fourth day:

Melon	Split pea	Nectarines	Antelope
Broiled goat	soup home-	fresh in sea-	stew
chops *or* eggs,	made w/out	son or home-	Baked squash
any style	meat stock	canned	Swiss chard
cooked in	cooked w/		
spring water or	grated car-		
oil	rot & parsley		
	or		
	Lobster &		
	sliced fresh		
	tomato		

Fifth morning:

Ground hippo gravy made w/tapioca flour & spring water	Invariably the beverage is spring water.
Sliced oranges *or* papaya	In the case of alternates both dishes are prepared. The alternates are to accommodate allergies not choice.

This menu is worked out scientifically to the Caspers' requirements. It is *not* a recommendation for general use or unknowing adaptation.

All home-canned fruits are put up without sweeteners in glass sealed with enamel-lined lids. Fish is simpler broiled or poached, in order to cut down on the number of substances used. However, fish is often fried using arrowroot or tapioca flours, and sesame or safflower cold-pressed oils employed rotationally. The children like it better cooked this way. As required and/or permitted, turkey, beef, lamb, potato, carrots, and green peas are reserved for dining out in restaurants or friends' homes.

One last item concerning the program: While on tour, the first sign that Billy is having an allergic reaction is that he loses his depth-perception. Del, his caddy, knows him so well that he can tell at once if Billy is in a playing mood. And the conversation is likely to be unintelligible to the gallery when this occurs.

"Bill, you let those hamburgers beat you."

A CASPER FAMILY PARTY MENU

It would be wrong to leave the reader feeling that the Randolph program cuts out all special dinners from the Casper menu. They have holiday dinners, birthday dinners, just as others do. One of their favorites is the "wheat" dinner. Only within the last year of the workout have they been able to have this. It does require advance planning. The menu must be set up and the required items must be "saved" in advance out of the regular diet. That is, if there is to be cake, wheat must be kept from the menu for at least four days before the dinner—the four days of rotation. In the Casper situation, where wheat is a reclaimed allergen, they wait *five* days. Many of the items on this menu are reclaimed allergens and require this five-day interval.

The Casper "party" menu contains fifteen food substances and is given herewith:

Party menu:

Spaghetti with game meat and organic-vegetable sauce
    (1)   wheat
    (2)   sesame
    (3)   elk
    (4)   celery
    (5)   tomato
    (6)   parsley
    (7)   onion (green)
Homemade sourdough bread served w/butter
            wheat (#1 above)
            butter (made from raw cream) (#13 below)
Organic-vegetable salad
    (8)   romaine
    (9)   avocado
    (10) cucumber
            celery, tomato, parsley (#4, 5, 6 above)
Salad dressing
            sesame oil (#2 above)
    (11) lemon
Cake and ice cream
    (12) egg
    (13) milk and cream
    (14) sugar
    (15) vanilla
            wheat (#1 above)

The spaghetti is made with a specially prepared sesame-gluten paste, smothered in a sauce made with ground beef, elk, moose, or buffalo to accommodate various individual needs. Everyone loves the homemade sourdough bread, and willingly goes without wheat for the required five days to earn the right to eat it. Granny or Shirley makes the bread from stoneground grain. The salad is romaine, avocado, cucumber, celery, tomato, and parsley, with an oil-lemon dressing. For dessert, they have cake specially prepared with unenriched flour and ice cream homemade from raw milk. Neither the cake filling nor the ice cream can contain cornstarch or corn syrup. Of course, the ice cream is the supreme delight. And this brings forth the troubles of milk.

The Casper family's workout in the program is such that milk now fits into one meal every five days. When the family was first tested, all except young Billy showed an allergy to milk. He could have cow's milk, but he could not and still cannot tolerate pasteurized enriched milk. Suspect is the vitamin used in enriched milk. It is thought to be a yeast product, and son Billy has a high sensitivity to yeast. Whenever raw milk is available, Billy does fine with it once every *four* days.

To many this will seem a simple enough meal. But served amid smiling children's faces, loving adults, and treat-hungry appetites, it is special indeed, and a gala occasion.

At school and Church functions, Granny and Shirley often close their eyes and trust, allowing the children to indulge in punch, miscellaneous cookies, and commercial ice cream. The children, except young Billy and Johnny, weather this departure from the program with only minor behavioral manifestations—provided it is not done too often. The salts jar usually comes down for the two boys, and oxygen is often needed to ward off their reaction.

Bill partakes of the party menu only when he is off tour and has time to recuperate from any possible ill effects. At this point in his workout the main offender for him in the party menu is sugar.

BILLY CASPER'S SCORECARD
(from PGA records)

Tournament	Score	Official Winnings		Tournaments Played				
		Year	To Date	In Money	Year	To Date	Year To Date	Won Year To Date
1955								
Western Open (First Money) (at Portland)	72, 71, 72, 72—287	$33.33						
Total for year		$3,253.82	$3,253.82	11	14	14	0	0
1956								
LaBatt Open	68, 68, 67, 71—274	$5,000						
Total for year		$18,733.41	$21,987.23	26	31	45	1	1
1957								
Phoenix Open	71, 65, 67, 68—271	$2,000						
Kentucky Derby Open	68, 68, 71, 70—277	4,300						
Total for year		$20,807.83	$42,795.06	21	34	79	2	3
1958								
Crosby National	71, 66, 69, 71—277	$4,000						
New Orleans Open	69, 70, 70, 69—278	2,800						
Buick Open	70, 73, 71, 71—285	9,000						
Havana International	66, 68, 72, 72—278	(Unofficial money only: Amount $2,400)						
Total for year		$41,323.75	$84,118.81	25	31	110	4	7

Tournament	Score	Official Winnings		In Money	Tournaments Played		Won	
		Year	To Date		In Year	To Date	Year	To Date
1959								
U.S. Open	71, 68, 69, 74—282	$12,000						
Portland Open	69, 64, 67, 69—269	2,800						
LaFayette Open	69, 64, 71, 69—273	2,000						
Mobile Open	71, 68, 68, 73—280	2,000						
Total for year		$33,899.39	$118,018.20	20	25	135	4	11
1960								
Portland Open	68, 67, 66, 65—266	2,500						
Hesperia Open	70, 68, 67, 70—275	2,000						
Orange County Open	70, 68, 69, 69—276	2,000						
Total for year		$31,060.83	$149,079.03	21	24	159	3	14
1961								
Portland Open	68, 71, 67, 67—273	3,500						
Total for year		$37,766.78	$186,845.81	24	26	185	1	15
1962								
Doral Open	70, 67, 75, 71—283	9,000						
Greensboro Open	69, 70, 68, 68—275	5,300						
500 Festival Open	66, 67, 67, 64—264	9,000						
Bakersfield Open	69, 71, 65, 67—272	6,400						
Total for year		$61,842.19	$248,688.00	21	25	210	4	19

Tournament	Score	Official Winnings		Tournaments Played			Won	
		Year	To Date	In Money	Year	To Date	Year	To Date
1963								
Crosby National	73, 65, 73, 74—285	5,300						
Insurance City Open	67, 68, 71, 65—271	6,400						
Total for year		$32,726.19	$281,414.19	19	21	231	2	21
1964								
Doral Open	70, 70, 67, 70—277	$ 7,500						
Colonial National	72, 67, 70, 70—279	14,000						
Seattle Open	68, 67, 66, 64—265	5,800						
Almaden Open	68, 70, 73, 68—279	3,300						
Total for year		$90,653.08	$372,067.27	26	32	263	4	25
1965								
Hope Desert Classic	70, 69, 67, 72—278	(unofficial in 1965. Amount $15,000)						
Western Open	70, 66, 70, 64—270	$11,000						
Insurance City Open	70, 72, 66, 66—274	11,000						
Sahara International	66, 66, 68, 69—269	20,000						
Total for year		$99,931.90	$471,999.17	27	31	294	4	29
1966								
San Diego Open	70, 66, 68, 69—268	$ 5,800						
U.S. Open*	69, 68, 73, 68—278	25,000						
Western Open	69, 72, 72, 70—283	20,000						
500 Festival Open	69, 70, 68, 70—277	16,400						
Total for year		$121,944.92	$593,944.09	21	25	319	4	33

Tournament	Score	Official Winnings		Tournaments Played				
		Year	To Date	In Money	Year	To Date	Won Year	Won To Date
1967								
Canadian Open	69, 70, 71, 69—279	$27,840						
Carling Open	74, 68, 70, 69—281	35,000						
Total for year		$129,423.23	$723,367.32	22	26	345	2	35
1968								
Los Angeles Open	70, 67, 68, 69—274	$20,000						
Greensboro Open	65, 67, 69, 66—267	27,500						
Colonial National	68, 71, 68, 68—275	25,500						
500 Festival Open	70, 71, 69, 70—280	20,000						
Hartford (Insur. City)	68, 65, 67, 66—266	20,000						
Lucky International Open	68, 65, 70, 66—269	20,000						
Total for year		$205,168.67	$904,805.51 †	21	23	368	6	45
1969 (to Febr. 23, 1969)								
Hope Desert Classic:	71, 68, 71, 69, 66—345	$20,000						
Total so far in 1969		$30,291.76	$910,919.80	6	6	374	1	46

* Playoff, one of the greatest moments of golf: Casper, 69; Palmer, 73.

† In 1968, the method of totaling money won was changed. This amount is the official sum of "Modern Era" wins, taken from the records of the PGA.